THE NEW BRITISH

The New British
The Impact of Culture and Community on Young Pakistanis

IKHLAQ DIN
University of Bradford, UK

ASHGATE

© Ikhlaq Din 2006

Ikhlaq Din has asserted his moral right under the Copyright, Designs and Patents Act, 1988, to be identified as the author of this work.

Published by
Ashgate Publishing Limited
Gower House
Croft Road
Aldershot
Hampshire GU11 3HR
England

Ashgate Publishing Company
Suite 420
101 Cherry Street
Burlington, VT 05401-4405
USA

Ashgate website: http://www.ashgate.com

British Library Cataloguing in Publication Data
Din, Ikhlaq
  The new british : the impact of culture and community on
  young Pakistanis
  1.Pakistanis - England - Bradford - Attitudes 2. Pakistanis
  - England - Bradford - Social conditions 3.Muslim youth -
  England - Bradford - Attitudes 4. Muslim youth - England -
  Bradford - Social conditions
  I.Title
  305.2'35'089914122'04281

Library of Congress Cataloging-in-Publication Data
Din, Ikhlaq, 1968-
  The new British : the impact of culture and community on young Pakistanis / by
Ikhlaq Din.
      p. cm.
  Includes bibliographical references and index.
  ISBN-13: 978-0-7546-4047-9
  ISBN-10: 0-7546-4047-7
  1. Pakistanis--Great Britain--Bradford (West Yorkshire)--Social conditions. 2.
Great Britain--Ethnic relations. 3. Pakistan--Emmigration and immigration. I. Title.

  DA125.S57D46 2006
  305.23089'914122042817--dc22

                                                                    2006018449
ISBN-10: 0 7546 4047 7
ISBN-13: 978-0-7546-4047-9

Printed and bound in Great Britain by Antony Rowe Ltd, Chippenham, Wiltshire.

Contents

Acknowledgements

I would like to thank the following for their support: Dr Paul Oliver and Dr Matthew Pearson. Most of all I would like to thank Professor Cedric Cullingford[1] for his guidance and support.

1 The data in *The New British* also appears in *Ethnicity and Englishness: Personal Identities in a Minority Community*, Cedric Cullingford, Cambridge Scholars Press Ltd, 2006.

Chapter 1

The Context of the Research

Introduction

This book examines the experiences of British-born young people of Pakistani origin and, who were between the ages of fourteen and nineteen living in Bradford at the time. The research had particular focus on the relationship between young boys/girls, their parents and the Pakistani community. It examined issues such as the experience of school, aspirations, identity, popular culture, the experience of community, relationships with parents and the tensions between Islam and culture. This book explores issues of power and control within this community; exploring the activities of individual lives. It examines the importance and the influence of culture in relation to Islam; and the role it plays in the wider group of the Pakistani community and specifically with the young people in Bradford, in terms of the distinctions between generations, i.e. how an 'alien' culture adapts to a new culture.

A number of studies have explored the extent of 'Asian' (or Pakistani) migration and settlement across various geographical towns and cities (see Khan, 1974, 1979; Anwar, 1979; Shaw, 1988, 1994; Werbner, 1990). Some have had a particular focus on employment and housing issues (in particular Dahya, 1974; Werbner and Anwar, 1991; Anwar, 1991). Measuring the economic position of communities is easier to determine; what is more difficult is to examine the experiences and attitudes of young people towards their parents/elders; their community and the wider British society.

There is an enormous amount of published work on the early immigrants (Rose et al, 1969; Dahya, 1974; Khan 1979). Rose et al (1969) is a good starting point for cultural studies relating to the Pakistani community. Rose explored issues such as the need to recruit labour immigrants to meet the needs of the British economy and the settlement process of the early immigrants in textile cities like Bradford. In addition he explored the problems encountered, such as obtaining suitable accommodation, access to public services, integration and the problems of adapting to a very different way of life. The experiences of families of early settlers joining their husbands in the United Kingdom have also, to an extent, been explored. This shows close-knit family ties which exist in Pakistani families, arranged marriages, biraderi and gender inequalities in Pakistani households (Khan, 1979).

There is a need to understand the viewpoints of young people themselves as opposed to their parents or elders 'speaking on their behalf'. This is often the case in most communities and this community is no exception. This was one flaw in the many reports that followed the disturbances in 1995 in Bradford and in the northern towns and cities in 2001. The views of the young people themselves were often overlooked. Where the opinions of parents and community elders have been aired publicly, for example during the Halal meat demonstrations or during the Rushdie affair, the opinions of young people have often been ignored or overlooked for the purposes of inquiries and reports. There is still a need to examine the attitudes of young people by using empirical evidence rather than relying on secondary sources or, worse, subjective opinions. This lack of empirical research has prevented a better understanding of the particular nature of the Pakistani community, or indeed a clearly defined minority group in England. Bradford has its own peculiarities but it can also be deemed typical of others. There is the inevitable complexity of the 'Pakistani community' that needs to be unravelled to provide a greater understanding of this community and, indeed, how we conduct ethnographic research into other minority and majority communities.

A major turning point was the disturbances in the Manningham area of Bradford during the summer of 1995. The disturbances marked a change as, until then, the Pakistani community had remained on the whole closed to the 'outside'. The disturbances, and the many reports that soon followed, drew attention to inter-generational conflict within the Pakistani community. However the *Bradford Commission report* into the 1995 disturbances concentrated mainly on the role of the local police in Manningham, rather than on the people and communities. When we actually look closer we know little about the community. The Bradford Commission unwittingly emphasized the need to conduct research on the second generation of Pakistani people in Bradford and their culture, to see whether this position has changed in contemporary Bradford and, if so, how it has changed. More specifically, there is a need to investigate the experiences and the attitudes of young Pakistani children living in Bradford, as an example of the wider community. Some of the later reports into the disturbances in 2001 highlighted issues of segregation and deprivation of some minority ethnic communities and, in particular, the Pakistanis.

The issue of intergenerational conflict or tensions is common in most communities (majority and minority) and this community is no exception. There is an assumption that the experience of different generations is similar in some respects and different in others. Some of the earlier findings still hold good but are to some extent mitigated by time, and the erosion of such extreme attitudes can be seen as defensiveness. We cannot, however, fully understand the present circumstances without taking into account the traditions and the experiences of the immigrants. This suggests that some things have changed the position of children of immigrants who are born and raised in Britain and the different levels of adjustment by different minority ethnic communities, i.e. Indian, Bangladeshi. Another issue brought to the attention of most was that of institutional racism. It was not deemed that it was only individuals who perpetrated racism but institutions also who had an important role to play.

There is another issue of importance surrounding 'ethnic data'. There are those who argue that we need statistics, for example as to the number of Pakistanis or Muslims living in the United Kingdom or in a particular city. Some of the problems are obvious because this is likely to produce an extensive breakdown; the Pakistani community (like others) is not homogeneous and there are enormous differences among 'Pakistanis' that include variations in language, culture, identity and religious differences. We need to be clear as to the purpose of such data and how it will be used. The danger is that information may be used simply to mark out distinctions (or differences between groups) based on ethnic and racial grounds.

Settlement of Pakistanis: Bradford

Bradford is often described as a multi-cultural city, which has a long history of people arriving from Asia, Europe and Africa. This trend has continued with the new arrivals such as asylum seekers coming from Eastern Europe and other parts of the world. Bradford is seen as a rich cultural capital of Britain. As a result of the settlement process, ethnically diverse communities have appeared. Some parts of Bradford are seen as 'Pakistani' or 'Asian' areas, for example the University ward; Great Horton, Lidget Green, Little Horton, West Bowling, Leeds Road, while closely surrounding districts such as Wibsey, Queensbury and Thornton are seen as very White/English areas. Other districts such as Thornbury are more 'mixed'. This should not suggest that areas are exclusively home to one minority ethnic group, some are mixed. The important point is that some residents of Bradford (and those outside of the district) make these distinctions based on ethnic or racial grounds. This does not suggest that Asians/Pakistanis live exclusively only in poor areas or deprived areas, for example the prosperous area of Heaton has a large number of Pakistani residents.

The overwhelming majority of Pakistanis (young and old) have an attachment to Bradford. For many older Pakistanis, who arrived in the late 1950s and early 60s, 'Bradford is Mirpur' is their 'home from home'. For the young generations of Pakistanis it is their home. Bradford is traditionally seen by Pakistanis as a good place to live, with relatively cheap housing and opportunities for business and enterprise that some young people wish to exploit. Something which was highlighted by young people was that Bradford had changed considerably since when their parents first arrived in the UK in the late 1950s and early 60s. One area where enormous change has occurred is in the employment market or the shortage of suitable jobs. For those who left school with few qualifications the textile industry was seen as secure long-term employment. The closing down of textile mills in the 1970s and 80s, which provided employment to thousands of newly arrived immigrant men, had an enormous effect on Bradford and its residents (a similar story to many other textile towns). New industries had not been developed to cater for those seeking employment.

Although Pakistani Muslims settled in various parts of the United Kingdom, Bradford still has one of the highest concentrations of Pakistani Muslims in the country (and more than any other Yorkshire and Humber region). Bradford is one of many towns and cities that have ethnically diverse populations in terms of religion as well such places as Tower Hamlets, Birmingham and Slough (National Census, 2001). The Bradford area also has one of the highest numbers of individuals who were born outside the European Union (National Census, 2001). The majority of the population of Bradford is White (78.3 per cent); Asians or Asian-British account for 18.9 per cent, of which 14.5 per cent are Pakistanis. In terms of religion, the majority of those in the district describe themselves as being Christian (60.1 per cent) and Muslims account for 16.1 per cent of the residents. However, a number of those in the district have 'no religion' (13.3 per cent) (National Census, 2001).

Social Exclusion in Bradford

After coming into power in 1997 the Labour Government made it a pledge to tackle social exclusion of young people by establishing the Social Exclusion Unit. This was a step in the right direction in tackling inequalities faced by young people. There is an enormous amount of literature which points to social exclusion of young people. For example the study by Britton et al (2002; JRF) found significant numbers of 16-17-year-olds disengaged from education, employment and training; many are unknown to the Careers Service and nearly half the sample had been excluded from school.

Furlong and Cartmel (2004) found that most young men had left school without any qualifications and had spent time on Youth Training, and the opportunities available tended to be temporary and short-term work. Young men were looking for job security (see also Johnson and Burden, 2003). Others point to the social exclusion and inequality faced by members of minority ethnic communities (Modood et al, 1997; Chahal, 2004). They are much more likely when compared to White groups to live in sub-standard housing in parts of inner cities, more likely to be unemployed or when employed to be in semi-skilled or unskilled occupations. They also face discrimination in other fields such as in education (Osler, 2002; Davis et al, 2002), health and social services (Mir, 2000; Vernon, 2002). This deprivation can also lead to poorer health outcomes: for example the actual prevalence of learning disabilities between years 5 and 34 among the minority ethnic groups is three times higher than compared to White groups (Emerson et al, 1997). This is related to social and economic deprivation (Emerson and Robertson, 2002).

Pakistani Muslims settled in various parts of the United Kingdom, Bradford has one of the highest concentrations of Pakistani/Muslims in the country (and more than any other Yorkshire and Humber region). Bradford is one of many towns and cities that have ethnically diverse populations in terms of religion as well as geographical location, for example Tower Hamlets, Birmingham and Slough (National Census, 2001). The Bradford area also has one of the highest numbers of individuals who were born outside the European Union (National Census, 2001). The total population of Bradford is 467,000, although more people leave than come to Bradford. The district has more births (88 per cent of Bradford's residents were born in the UK) than deaths as well as continuing immigration, particularly from South Asia, which adds to the population. The majority of the population of Bradford is White (78.3 per cent); Asians or Asian-British account for 18.9 per cent, of which 14.5 per cent are Pakistanis.

Bradford has a young population compared to the national trend. The district has 33,240 (7 per cent) 0-4-year-olds compared to the national average of 6 per cent. This also applies to the 5-15 year-olds: the district has 76,097 (16 per cent) compared to the national average of 14 per cent (National Census, 2001). This trend is likely to continue. The Muslim population of the UK stands at 687,592 (National Census, 2001) (originated from Mirpur, Pakistan). Further, the UK Muslim population is increasing with large numbers of young people, 33.8 per cent of Muslims are aged 0-15 years compared to the national average 20.2 per cent. Fifty per cent of Muslims are aged 25 years or less compared to the national average of 31 per cent (National Census, 2001).

A total of 35.1 per cent of the district's population have no qualifications, compared to the English average of 29.1 per cent. Bradford also has a lower than average number of people qualified to degree level or higher when compared to the English average (15.9 per cent and 19.8 per cent respectively) (National Census, 2001). Bradford and district has the region's third largest economy and accounts for 9 per cent of all employment (BMDC, 2003). A total of 56.5 per cent of the district's population is employed, compared to the English average of 60.6 per cent. In total 4.4 per cent of the population is unemployed, which is higher than the English average of 3.4 per cent. In terms of occupation concentration Muslims tend to be found in manufacturing, distribution and hotels and restaurants trades and are less likely to be in professional-type occupations compared both to the White British and other minority groups, for example the Indians (National Census, 2001). Muslims have lower rates of participation in employment than Whites but are more likely to be self-employed (Annual Local Area Labour Force Survey, 2001/02).

The Index of Multiple Deprivation 2004 shows that Bradford is the fifth most deprived local authority in England. The total number of people unemployed in the district is 8,307 (rate of 2.9 per cent) this is higher compared to the national rate of 2.4 per cent. There are gender differences; the number of male claimants in March 2005 was 6,443 showing a rate of 4.3 per cent compared to the national rate of 3.4 per cent. Compare this to 1,864 (1.3 per cent) of females unemployed, which is the same rate as the national average (1.3 per cent). There are significant differences in the unemployment rate by Ward. For example the Bowling (5.5 per cent), Little Horton (6.2 per cent), Toller (4.7 per cent), Undercliffe (5.1 per cent) and University (4.2 per cent) all have higher unemployment rates than the Bradford district average of 2.9 per cent (BMDC, 2005). These Wards also have a high number of minority ethnic populations. The unemployment rate differs enormously among the Bradford population. Pakistanis are more likely to be unemployed than the White population but also when compared to other minority ethnic groups. Youth unemployment in Bradford accounts for 33.4 per cent of all unemployment; this is higher than both the regional (32.8 per cent) and UK (30.7 per cent) figures (BMDC, 2005). Bradford also has a higher than the English average of owner-occupied properties (71.7 per cent and 68.9 per cent respectively) (National Census, 2001). Pakistani households are larger compared to the national picture (4.7 and 2.3 persons respectively).

The Index of Multiple Deprivation 2000 shows that Bradford district is one of the most deprived wards in the UK. There is enormous evidence that links deprivation to poor health outcomes. For example life expectancy in Bradford (73.5) is lower than compared to the national average (75.2). Bradford has a significantly higher rate of cancers (142.9 per 100,000 under-75s) than England (130.6) as a whole. The mortality rate from circulatory diseases in people aged under 75 per 100,000 population in Bradford (146.4) is also higher than the national average (120.4). The Bradford district has the second highest infant mortality rate with 8.4 deaths per 1,000 live births compared to the national average (5.7).

Bradford is a centre of enterprise and entrepreneurship and is home to hundreds of Asian/Pakistani businesses. Pakistani business has come a long way since the late 1950s and a far cry from when Rose et al (1969) reported a small number of Pakistani-owned businesses in Bradford. All kinds of goods and services are provided by Pakistani businesspeople. Many are small traders and run by family members which ensures stability and continuity, as well as keeping costs down. Wages are often kept low because family members are at times paid less, especially when the business may not be doing well. It is also about reliability, especially when the owner may be on holiday the son or the brother will take charge. All members of the family own a share in the business.

Much of this has been possible because of the work ethic of Pakistanis and the desire to succeed, which is as strong as when they first arrived in the UK. Most work very long hours and it is not untypical for the Pakistani greengrocer to be up at 4am, visit the wholesaler, open by 8am and remain open till 9 in the evening or the Pakistani-owned newsagent to work from 7am to 8pm. Never mind the Pakistani-owned corner shop which stereotypically 'never seems to close' and sells everything and anything. This is not unique to Bradford but is typical of many towns and cities across the UK.

9/11 and 7/7

Two events will mark a new turning point in world history and international relations: the 9/11 attacks and the 7/7 London bombings. For some these events illustrate the rise of militancy and the determination to challenge this emergence.

On September 11, 2001 a series of suicide attacks against the United States occurred. According to the 9/11 Commission Report, 19 men affiliated with Osama bin Laden and Al-Qaeda hijacked four US domestic commercial airliners. Twenty-seven members of Al-Qaeda attempted to take part in the 9/11 attacks. At the end only 19 took part; the other would-be hijackers are commonly referred to as the 20th hijackers. As a result two planes were crashed into the World Trade Center in Manhattan, New York City. The third aircraft crashed into the US Department of Defense headquarters, the Pentagon, in Arlington County, Virginia. The fourth aeroplane crashed into a field in Somerset County, Pennsylvania. The official record shows that a total of 2,986 people died in the attacks. The 9/11 attacks were the largest suicide bombs in history. The 9/11 attacks had severe repercussions on social and economic life. The large number of public-safety workers killed was a result of risking their lives to save fellow Americans. Since 9/11 public reaction has lead to a surge in patriotism in the USA not seen since the Second World War. At the same time it has also led to a rise in hate-crime against Middle Eastern people. There was also economic repercussions for the USA and world financial markets. The New York Stock Exchange, the American Stock Exchange and NASDAQ remained closed until 17th September because of the damage caused to the telephone exchange facility near the World Trade Center. Share prices were also hit: the Dow Jones Industrial Average (DJIA) stock market fell 684 points or 7.1%, to 8920, its biggest-ever one-day decline. Air travel was seriously affected remaining closed several days after 9/11. The repercussions of the bombings are still felt today; the US airline industry has not fully recovered. There have been many 'conspiracy theories' that cast speculation concerning the execution of the 9/11 attacks that Al-Qaeda did not carry out the attacks but some other unknown group. This remains a speculation (Wikipedia, 2005). To combat further attacks on the US, President George W. Bush with the support of the United Nations took the brave step by declaring war on international terrorism.

On Thursday 7th July 2005 four suicide bombers struck in central London killing 56 and injuring a further 700. The bombers coordinated to cause maximum destruction to the public and the transport system. Three of the bombs went off at 0850 BST on underground trains immediately outside Liverpool Street and Edgware Road stations, and on another travelling between King's Cross and Russell Square. The fourth bomber struck an hour later on a double-decker bus in Tavistock Square, near King's Cross. These were the first suicide bombings in Western Europe: Al-Qaeda claimed responsibility (BBC News, 7/7/2005), although initial reports suggested that a power surge in the Underground grid had caused explosions in power circuits. The Metropolitan Police Commissioner Sir Ian Blair confirmed within hours that it was 'probably a major terrorist attack'. Three of the four alleged suicide bombers were British-born (Wikipedia, 2005). This sent shockwaves throughout the UK that British-born Pakistanis could perpetrate such an act. This has also resulted in tensions between the White/English and Pakistani/Muslim communities in the UK. On the 21st July 2005 a second series of four explosions occurred in London. All four bombs remained undetonated and fortunately there were no fatalities. All the suspected bombers from this failed attempt were arrested by the police (Wikipedia, 2005). This is not to overlook the fact that there have been many bombings on mainland Europe.

Chapter 2

Methods:
Conducting Research on the Pakistani Community

This research is designed to fill a significant gap in a sensitive issue and is focused on a particular community rather than generalizing about the British/Pakistani population. At the same time the findings allow for general conclusions to apply to the Pakistani population as a whole and those residing in other towns and cities in England. Both quantitative (questionnaires) and qualitative (in-depth semi-structured interviews) were used. The data was collected in the late 1990s and in three stages; in-depth semi-structured interviews were followed by a questionnaire and then by further semi-structured interviews. The sample takes into account the age, gender and socio-economic background. A traditional sampling frame was not used, taking into account the sensitive nature of the research. Instead opportunistic sampling was used. All secondary schools and further education colleges in the City of Bradford were given the opportunity to participate in the research. The intention was to ask as many schools/colleges and young people to participate in the survey as possible.

An initial letter was sent to all comprehensive schools within the City of Bradford that have pupils aged between the ages of fourteen to nineteen. This included state, public, single-sex, co-educational, religious schools and the local Colleges within the Bradford district. It was not enough to adhere to the standard approaches of semi-structured interviews (although the ethics of consistency were maintained) since the overall concern was to enable the sample to talk with openness and freedom. This entailed some degree of informality and flexibility. The questionnaires and the interviews were conducted at a number of locations around Bradford. Given limited access from schools and community centres, and given the sensitivity of the issues and the need for 'insider' access, it was necessary to make use of every opportunity to gather information and to improvise whilst maintaining the vigorous sense of empirical data. To be considered part of this community created a sense of openness and trust. On occasions the young people used the word 'apna' (Pakistani),

'you know how it is being an *apna*' (girl, age 19)

It was crucial to gain the confidence and respect of the young people as well understanding some of the issues faced by them in this particular community,

'You know what they say' (girl, age 14)

The young people felt comfortable about being interviewed and regarded the researcher as an 'apna' and part of the Pakistani community. It was significant that these young people considered the researcher as 'one of them' rather than as an 'outsider'. There can be problems; a respondent may feel hindered or reluctant to talk about their community and may well feel that a researcher from outside the community would be better. While others (as in this case) the young people feel comfortable to talking to 'one of theirs'. Some issues were much easier to discuss with someone from their own community, such as racism and being called racist names where it would be difficult for someone who is from outside the community to understand the hurt felt upon hearing those words.

Much has been written about class, gender and language 'matching' respondents with interviewers while conducting research. Being 'ethnically-matched' often allows the initial access to those being researched, however, they may not always be appropriate. We need to be aware of others that are equally important such as caste matching, sect matching and importantly region matching (such as those having origins from Mirpur or from Karachi). The 'region matching' ensures that the researcher understands some aspects of the participant's background, his/her culture, norms and traditions to provide some basis for dialogue and understanding; this is especially true when interviewing older Pakistanis (or Asians). These are important in order to create a dialogue between the respondent and the interviewer. Data collection is much more than just asking questions.

In terms of the sample, 22 semi-structured interviews were conducted with 13 boys and 9 girls. In terms of age, four 14 year-olds were interviewed followed by those aged 15 (three respondents); aged 16 (four respondents); aged 17 (six respondents); aged 18 (two respondents) and aged 19 (three respondents). In addition to this a questionnaire was used. The questionnaire was distributed by using two methods; in schools by teachers (78) and by hand (336) by the researcher. The questionnaires that were distributed by the researcher were given out in a number of locations around Bradford. A total of five hundred questionnaires were distributed which produced a response rate of 82 per cent (414). Although the difference was small, slightly more females than boys completed the questionnaire (51 per cent and 49 per cent respectively). In terms of age the spread was as follows; 14 year olds (33), 15 year olds (47), 16 year olds (62), 17 year olds (119), 18 year olds (130) and 19 year olds (23).

The majority of young people who took part in the research came from manual backgrounds. Most fathers were employed in textiles, restaurants, as taxi drivers or were self-employed. It was common for some respondents' mothers to have several jobs, i.e. some worked in the family business while others did tailoring and packing work from home, often subsidizing the family income. The majority of respondents' parents had qualifications in Urdu but few had any formal qualifications in English. This applied both to the father and the mother. The parents of the respondents in the sample had all immigrated from Mirpur in Pakistan in the late 1950s and the early 1960s.

The questionnaire was preceded by in-depth semi-structured interviews which allowed for a number of themes and issues to be developed into a questionnaire. This allowed a larger number of young people to take part in the research. The interview schedule, like the questionnaire, was kept simple and easy to understand and awkward questions were avoided. The interview was an informal chat. Although a topic guide, with a pre-set of questions was developed it was rarely used. The topic guide was quickly put aside. The young people set the direction of the interview. Questions were asked on age, present course, intended destination, career aspirations, occupation and qualifications of mother and father. Issues relating to identity, popular culture, Islam/culture, relationships with parents and the biraderi, marriage and sub-culture were raised.

On making contact the researcher explained the purpose of the research; what would become of the data collected and that it would include publications. They were happy that their point of view would be aired. Often the interviewee is unclear of what is expected of them, or indeed how to answer questions. Interviews are often conducted on a 'question-answer' basis that allows a little flexibility to suit the needs of the research so that data is manageable. In most cases a topic guide is devised and used in a structured way (we talk about the interviewee leading the interview and airing his/her point of view but it rarely happens). There are particular problems when interviewing older Pakistanis. A structured 'question-answer' format does not work in most cases. The interview ideally should be along the lines of a 'semi-structured discussion' or a narrative. Some would argue this might result in asking leading questions but at the generic level the topic guide is a set of leading questions devised by researchers. It is important that young people (or any other group of respondents) are listened to,

> 'I think that's why I enjoyed the interview that you were sat there asking me these questions and you were listening to me what I was saying' (boy, age 17)

These young people were open and willing to express their attitudes and discuss their experiences, which formed an important insight into the lives of young Pakistanis. Their experiences and the experiences of others, friends, family and relatives were part of a uniform line of reasoning and argument. It was equally important to select an environment where the young person felt comfortable. The interviews were conducted at various locations including libraries, educational institutions and community centres. Some interviews were conducted outside on a bench while others were interviewed on a grass verge. Although these settings were often noisy, with the sound of traffic in the background, the young people felt relaxed. Other interviews were conducted in the canteen at various times and locations.

Some issues are a common concern to all groups and communities that researchers need to be aware of when conducting research, such as the purpose of the research, while others are more specific to some communities. Some commonly used research methods are rarely applicable when dealing with participants who are Pakistani, particularly older Pakistanis. The assumption that 'one research method suits all communities' does not apply. What then are some of the more important issues that researchers need to be aware of?

Conducting research on the 'Pakistanis'

The type of research methods that will be used needs careful consideration before being put into practice, as some are clearly more unsuitable than others. For example, focus group interviews can be an important source of gathering data but they should only be used in exceptional circumstances for Pakistani participants if at all. Anonymity is difficult to ensure when participants may know each other. Those taking part may live on the same street or they could be related. The location of the focus group also needs to be carefully planned. Holding a focus group in the local community centre can be unsuitable. 'Asian' community centres tend to be used mainly by men and Pakistani women are often reluctant to attend unfamiliar or male-orientated surroundings.

Using questionnaires can also be unsuitable when conducting research with older Pakistanis, many of whom are illiterate or have limited skills, not only in English but also in Urdu (a large number of Pakistanis in the UK speak Mirpuri, a dialect of Urdu). It is practically impossible to devise a questionnaire to complement all the languages and dialects spoken. Questionnaires can be used with younger Pakistanis but only when it includes other qualitative methods such as semi-structured interviews.

There are other issues that need to be taken into account. The date and time of the interview is important. For example researchers must avoid making contact with Pakistani participants at Namaz time (there are five Namaz a day at various times), Thursday evenings when special prayers are said and during Jumma (Friday prayers held during early afternoon). While other special occasions take place once a year one also needs to be aware of Ramzan (Fasting) and Eid. This is particularly busy time for Pakistanis and researchers should avoid making contact during this time or even better avoid any contact with this sample group. A letter instead could be sent explaining that the research team wish to conduct an interview with a member of the household but feel that it is inappropriate to arrange this during Ramzan and will make contact after Eid. If the initial contact is made face-to-face and time for Namaz happens to overlap with the interview (something that may be unavoidable) then it is expected that the researcher who is part of this community that he/she should join in the Namaz. While a researcher who is not part of the community should be aware of the time of the Namaz and allow time accordingly. It is important to go prepared and adapt as circumstances change. Something that can be overlooked by researchers is to realize that not all Pakistanis (or indeed all Asians) are the same and who will have the same practices.

It is essential to understand 'Pakistani etiquette'. If the researcher conducting the interview is from outside the community then it advisable for him/her to talk to one of his/her Pakistani colleagues to ask questions and explain the 'do's and don'ts'. The interview starts when the first contact is made. When entering the participant's house it is polite to offer to remove one's shoes and exchange salaam (greetings) with the participant. In the case of a male researcher, a firm handshake with the male participant is normal. If there are males present the researcher must shake hands and exchange salaam in order of importance, starting with the eldest first. If there are females present then the male researcher must exchange salaam first with the lady(s) and then by shaking hands, starting with the eldest male. In the case of a female researcher, she must salaam the lady(s) first, normally a handshake and/or hug, followed by salaam with any males present. It is customary to sit down without being asked by the participant, since the guest should treat the 'home like his home'. This is followed by further customary salaams and asking about one's health and about any children the participant may have (if the researcher is aware of this). Other common topics of discussion are Pakistan and current affairs.

Where the interview is not gender-matched (for example, male researcher and female interviewee) then under no circumstance should he ask questions about the participant's female siblings. In this case the male researcher should only speak when he is spoken to. This is made easier when a female researcher interviews a male participant. She is often treated as a 'daughter' and most issues can be discussed such as siblings. As part of this trust building process, the researcher must be able to talk about what is regarded as being 'personal information' in the western sense i.e. talking about one's marital status, siblings, background of the spouse and parents is common. It is customary to be open and genuine in a community where little is kept hidden. In this situation both the participant and the researcher are being interviewed by each other.

Building rapport between the researcher and the participant is essential. To make them feel at ease and relaxed, and to encourage a natural discussion between two individuals, cultural sensitivity is paramount. Rapport means that the researcher is often asked questions about his family including his/her age, whether or not he/she is married and if applicable, if he/she has any children, names of his/her parents and grandparents, where they come from in Pakistan, names of uncles and aunts and what they do. Hospitality is an integral part of the Pakistani community, taking tea and even dinner should be accepted when offered. Hospitality should not be refused since it is likely to cause offence. If the researcher is younger than the participant then he/she should serve tea again starting with the eldest male/female first. This is all part of the introduction stage.

Most people have some experience of being interviewed, often in a job interview situation but fewer people are interviewed for research purposes. For most it is a totally new and alien situation. Often the research participant is unsure in terms of how to answer questions. Others are 'guessing' the correct answer or what the researcher wants to hear. This is similar to being in a classroom situation where the child is second-guessing what the teacher wants to hear. Answering questions, often in a structured way, is difficult for most and the researcher needs to explain and discuss this with the participant.

The researcher should also ask the participant in what form he/she requires further correspondence to be made, for example by letter and/or telephone or some may even prefer to be sent an e-mail instead (depending on the literacy levels of the individual), while others may prefer to receive communication to be made through a third party. It is also important to know which dialect the participant speaks and to provide correspondence in that language or dialect. Normally any communication between the researcher and the participant should be in English, Urdu or in any other dialect (letters etc.) and also on audio-tape in case the participant is unable to read. It is important to be aware of language issues and the many dialects spoken. For example most Pakistanis speak Azad Kashmiri Punjabi. The golden rule is that each participant will be different. And the researcher needs to do 'research on the participant'.

Researchers need to be aware of other issues. For example how the sample group would be contacted raises further issues, confidentiality is one of these. If contact is made by telephone what would happen if the 'elder' answers, which is what normally happens amongst the Pakistanis? The 'elder' can be the father, mother, brother, the husband or the in-laws. He/she must be convinced of the purpose of research and would normally request to read the topic guide and/or even meet the researcher. It is this person who will often grant access to their family members as he/she is the spokesperson for the family. The question is, who is consenting to take part, the elder or the person concerned? Participants such as unmarried girls and spouses from Pakistan are particularly difficult to recruit. Taking into account the above concerns, for most it is impolite to simply telephone and introduce the research. Whenever possible the initial contact should be made face-to-face, where potential participants can put a face to the name and the purpose of the research can be explained.

The place of the interview is crucial. If the interview is arranged to take place in the home of the participant then researchers need to be aware that family members could come into the room. What if they decide to stay and contribute? It is not acceptable to ask family members to leave the room or indeed, ask to be left alone while the interview is being conducted. This would go against the cultural norms of the Pakistani community where secrecy is frowned upon. The researcher is a guest and conducting the interview at a place where the participant will feel comfortable and at ease is crucial. These circumstances can be awkward for the participant where he/she may feel cajoled or obliged into continuing the interview (not by the researcher) but by the 'third party' present. In this case the researcher should allow the interview to be rearranged and even encourage this to take away the responsibility from the participant, particularly when the spouse is present.

It is normally made clear at the outset that the interview will be conducted in private to ensure confidentiality but the reality is often different. Researchers need to be careful when asking for consent from the participant in the presence of third parties. It is common for an 'unwanted guest' such as a relative to be visiting or a family member to be present at the time of the interview. The question is whether the interview should take place. The 'unwanted guest' could contribute to the interview, and to whatever is being discussed. The focus of the interview can often change depending on the contribution made by the 'unwanted guest', but how valid is the data collected in these circumstances; is it ethical and is it confidential? Some would say the interview should be rearranged for another time. However, to do so we would be overlooking the norms of the community in question. The situation is culturally specific. We think the 'unwanted guest' can be excused from the interview room but this would be from a western perspective whereas in this community whoever is present at the time can remain present and is allowed to contribute. In fact it is not considered polite to ask the 'guest' to leave and should not be suggested to the participant; after all the researcher is also a guest in the participant's house. The 'interview' is often along the lines of a communal discussion as opposed to being one to one. Western research methods are sometimes not applicable when conducting research on the Pakistani community.

Leaving the house after the interview can raise other issues such as prying neighbours and relatives, who often reside nearby, as is the case of the Pakistanis. The intrusive neighbour, who enquires about the researcher, can lead to divulging the nature of the interview unwillingly and in some cases the participant should not be interviewed. As pointed out earlier, the place of the interview should be left to the discretion of the participant. Another alternative may be to conduct a telephone interview. This interview should take place after the researcher has met and introduced the research to the participant and consent has been obtained. Researchers often require a consent form to be completed by the participant so that the participant understands the research. This may be problematic; especially for those who are unable to read the form as in most cases the consent form will be in English. Consent forms should be available in Urdu (or any other Asian language) and importantly also recorded on audio-tape so that the participant can listen to what is written on the consent form.

The post-interview stage is often overlooked yet it is crucial in building trust between researchers and the community. In some cases it is not acceptable to simply conduct the interview and leave without further contact of some kind. It is not uncommon, when interviewing older Pakistanis or those who have limited language skills in English, to ask for help of some kind. Usually the individual asks the researcher to complete official forms such as for Department of Work and Pensions or the respondent may ask for advice, in terms of what benefits he/she maybe entitled to. The researcher is seen as someone in authority, who has a certain level of education and who is in a position to help. It is expected that the researcher will provide help if asked.

'Suspicion' of researchers generally is a common problem and perhaps the major obstacle of all is one of access to the community. 'Gatekeepers' are often used to access tight-knit and closed communities. It is left to these people to supposedly 'open up' access for researchers. Gatekeepers often have a certain amount of social standing in their own communities. They are used to make the initial contact with potential participants and are often used in the recruiting process. Researchers have to be careful when they use gatekeepers for research purposes, since using them can lead to an unrepresentative sample. These individuals are often self-elected, biraderi elders who uphold the norms of their biraderi. Gatekeepers 'vet' the research and they decide whether they should allow access to individuals. Participants that are selected by gatekeepers are often 'hand picked'. Others considered as being 'unsuitable', such as separated/divorced women, are overlooked. It is essential to include these groups to ensure validity and also to ensure the views of those already marginalized can air their opinions. In these cases could the validity of the data be upheld? It is argued that we need to 'by-pass' community elders and use opportunistic sampling to recruit individuals. We also need to remember that sometimes problems of gaining access can be put down to research that is not relevant to those being researched. Often unrealized is that 'Asian' or 'Pakistani' researchers who are part of the community can also experience problems in gaining access to individuals/groups.

This leads us to another issue, an important one; who conducts the research? On research that examines minority ethnic communities there is a need to have researchers who are part of those communities under investigation. This has to be more than just using 'session researchers' who only conduct the interviews and then pass the transcripts onto the research team. This creates particular problems, especially when the interview is in Punjabi and then translated into English. This process loses much of the dynamics of the interview, unless researchers are able to understand not only what is being said, but also the community they are part of. Making sense of individuals who participate, and the communities they are a part of, takes an enormous amount of time.

For researchers who are not part of the Pakistani community it is difficult to undertake a research project for a short period of time and attempt to understand the community. It is difficult for some to understand the community even when they are part of it. Some say those outside the community can be more objective. Issues such as racism, and how it affects minorities in any given situation, such as when applying for jobs or accessing services, or indeed, simply walking down the street and someone makes a racist comment, are much harder to understand, never mind what the Asian or the Black person will feel upon hearing those comments.

Participants will also want to know what will happen to the research once it has been completed, in terms of dissemination. Writing reports and presenting the findings at conferences is for academic purposes but, importantly, researchers need to ask the participants how they would like the research to be disseminated so it is presented in a helpful way to them. 'Mini' conferences should be held followed by workshops, where all those who participated are invited to the event as well as other interested parties. These events should be held in the local neighbourhoods where the participants were drawn from. This should encourage the invitees to talk about the research and its implications. This also gives researchers the opportunities to explain the purpose of research and the possible benefits. The workshops are ideal to get a flavour of how relevant the research was to those taking part (since there would be gap between taking part and the dissemination activities), what worked well and, of course, what worked less well. If the participants have limited literacy skills, it is important to have interpreters available so the participants are in a position to contribute to the event in a positive and a constructive way. Disseminating research in this way allows a partnership to develop between researchers and the 'researched community'.

The final report should also be made available in Urdu and any other language/ dialect, depending on the ethnic background of the participants and importantly individual preference. It should also be available on audio-tape so that individuals with limited language skills can listen to the findings.

Summary

Research has to be relevant to the individuals who take part in order to engage them in the research process; this in turn will help participants understand the purpose of the research. It is not always clear, by those taking part, how the research is designed to benefit them directly. At worse some may feel that they are under-scrutiny or examination and can lead them to become defensive and closed. Building trust between those conducting the research, and those who are researched, is crucial (as well those who are funding the research). This is more so when conducting research on a tight-knit community, particularly on those groups that are often overlooked because of access problems.

Chapter 3

The Land of Dreams

Immigration

The religious, cultural and socio-economic position of Pakistani immigrants from Pakistan before their arrival into the United Kingdom is essential in understanding many of the attitudes of the community. Despite the geographical and cultural distance between the UK and Pakistan, there is still a major and ongoing influence from Pakistan because so many people travel back for visits, thus maintaining ties with relatives. Sometimes these trips are forced on people by their parents, such as when young people are sent back to Pakistan for an 'arranged' marriage. The context of both past and present influences the culture of individuals.

Britain has a long history of White and non-White immigration to its shores. The presence of Asians in Britain can be dated back to the seventeenth century (Fryer, 1984; Visram, 1986). Indians began coming to the UK from the early part of the twentieth century as seamen (Aurora, 1976; Desai, 1963) and settled in areas such as Birmingham (Rose et al, 1969). Others, mainly White people, arrived from Europe and Eastern Europe. The numbers increased dramatically, especially after the Second World War. Most escaped to avoid to persecution (Jackson, 1963). The mass migration of non-White workers started more slowly but during the 1950s increased substantially in the number of migrants from the West Indies. Although mass migration from India and Pakistan began from 1945 it also reached a high level from 1960 onwards (Anwar, 1995).

After the separation of East and West Pakistan (later Bangladesh and Pakistan) in 1947 from India, Mirpur became one of the three districts of Azad 'Free' Kashmir (Rose et al, 1969) and the majority of Pakistanis came from this region (Shaw, 2001). The majority of Pakistanis who settled in the UK resided in Bradford and Birmingham (Dahya, B., 1972-3; Shaw, 1988, 2000; Werbner, 1990). This involved a large-scale movement of people, under arrangements with the British government, Indian and Pakistani leaders (Allen, 1971; Taylor, 1976). This movement signified deep-rooted tensions between the different religious groups, Hindus, Sikhs and Muslims and their different ideas of nationalism.

There were several major reasons for the partition. Robinson (1993) argues that Muslim separatism was fostered both by the political needs of the British and by those of Hindus and Muslims. According to Robinson this was important because the religious differences that separated Muslims from the Hindus were fundamental. For example, Hindus worshipped idols whereas Muslims abhorred them. Hindus had many gods; the Muslims have one God. This created tension between the Hindu population and the Muslims who were in the minority. In addition, Muslims feared that the Hindu majority would not only interfere with Muslim religious practices, such as cow-sacrifices, but also religious differences would lead to discrimination against them in wider secular fields such as in education and in employment (Robinson, 1993; Brown and Foot, 1994).

After independence Pakistan went through a number of social changes. This included, for example, the spread of primary school education, and especially Islamic education and ideas of nationalism with reference to Kashmir. However, progress on the whole was slow, and unemployment was high (Rose et al, 1969; Taylor, 1976; Holmes, 1991). An illustration of poverty in Pakistan in the 1940s and the 1950s was the low literacy rate, and the poor provision of schooling (Braham, 1992). Due to high levels of poverty within the district of Mirpur only a small number of young children entered secondary schooling and less than half stayed on at the age of fifteen. Thus, it is not surprising that the majority of the immigrants who came to Britain were illiterate (Khan, 1979; Kannon, 1978). It was estimated that unemployment was 7.4 million at the end of 1964 (Economist Intelligence Unit, 1966). According to the speech made by the President of Pakistan, Ayub Khan, at the time the per capita income was only £30 per annum (Rose et al, 1969).

One significant factor that resulted in the migration of Pakistanis to the UK was the Pakistani Government's decision to build the world's largest hydroelectric earth dam at Mangla, which was constructed during the late 1950s and the early 1960s. As a result it submerged two hundred and fifty villages in the district of Mirpur and displaced approximately one hundred thousand people. As a result of the dam a new Mirpur city emerged at the side of the lake, which replaced the old Mirpur town. It acted as an impetus for Pakistani immigrants to come to Britain. Other displaced families were allocated land in the state of Punjab (Taylor, 1976; Holmes, 1991; Anwar, 1998).

There is a suggestion that many Pakistanis who came to the United Kingdom may have been reluctant migrants. On the one hand this may have been forced migration, but on the other it was opportunistic in terms of the benefits to be gained in coming to the United Kingdom. Peterson (1958) has described this as an 'impelled-flight type' migration. It is important to remember that immigrants who were driven out of their villages were psychologically different from those immigrants who came to Britain in search of new opportunities. It can be argued that the reason for the immigration was both economic and caste driven, which largely explains why the majority of immigrants who came to the United Kingdom belonged to lower castes, for example, Morchis (shoesmith) and Majaars (landless labour).

In reality, there were few economic reasons to encourage Pakistani men to stay in Mirpur or indeed Pakistan (Khan, 1979; Holmes, 1991; Lewis, 1994). To those who had relatives or fellow kinsmen who were already settled in the UK, unlimited opportunities proved to be an important deciding factor in chain migration. Another motive for lower caste families to immigrate was free 'vilayati' (English) education could improve the status of an individual as well as that of the family, whereas lower caste groups had always been subjugated by those higher than them and never had the opportunity to climb up the social hierarchy (Kannon, 1978).

A large number of immigrants, who originated from Mirpur, came from families who were connected with the land; the majority were small peasant farmers or landless labourers (Taylor, 1976; Lewis, 1994). Dahya found that two-thirds of the two hundred respondents interviewed had been farming their family's land prior to migration. Furthermore, nearly half had been in the Armed Forces or had served in the Merchant Navy. The survey by John Goodall (1968), of Pakistani men living in Huddersfield, showed that the majority of men had come from land-owning castes but their holdings had been so small as to make them almost landless i.e. they owned only a small plot of arable land (Rose et al, 1969; Lewis, 1994).

Roger Ballard argued that the early immigrants were drawn from peasant families with limited land holdings who could use overseas earnings to redeem mortgaged land, as well as buy more to provide sisters with dowries, to build new houses and to purchase agricultural implements (Rapoport et al, 1982). This had a cost to those living in Britain since most of the savings were sent to those relatives still left behind. They had to do without material things such as televisions. However, not all migrants who came to Britain were small farmers. A small number of urban educated middle-class migrants also arrived in Britain in the 1960s (Braham, 1992).

Early employment

There were strong 'push and pull' factors that attracted migrants to Great Britain, namely economic growth and underemployment (Anwar, 1993). The post-war period had left Great Britain, especially the industrial areas of the country, with acute labour shortages. The situation was not eased by thousands of servicemen killed during the Second World War and the fact that many thousands of families emigrated to countries such as Australia and Canada (Wrench and Solomos, 1993). At the time there was a massive backlog of industrial projects to be completed, the re-structuring of the country and the public services that had been destroyed during the War and the other plans that were in the Government pipeline, such as the creation of the National Health Service (Hiro, 1991).

Despite the large influx of migrants arriving into the United Kingdom from Eire, the problems of acute labour shortages affected British industry throughout the 1960s. The Government looked towards the British colonies in search of extra labour resources. The proposed National Health Service and the London Transport employees were largely recruited from the West Indies (Rose et al, 1969; Modood, 1997). This provided Great Britain with a reserve army of labour which was vast and cheap and which was only too willing to meet the needs of the British economy (Bhat and Ohri, 1988; Wrench and Solomos, 1993). It was also the result of the British Government's willingness to accept large numbers of Asians into the UK (Allen, 1971).

It was left to free-market forces to determine the number of immigrants entering the United Kingdom. Some British companies took the lead by advertising for workers in India and Pakistan (Anwar, 1998). Immigration was linked to Britain's imperial past, where communities of South Asian settlers in Britain are a reminder that the empire connoted a system of economic, ideological and cultural linkages forged over a period of some four centuries (Rich, 1994). The legacy of British Colonial rule determined the type of employment and industry in which such immigrants would be placed in the United Kingdom (Rose et al, 1969).

There are many studies that have shown the desire among Asian or Pakistani migrants to return 'home' after they have secured their financial position (see Dahya, 1974; Khan, 1974; Anwar, 1979). However, for most rural Pakistanis, vilayat (Britain) was considered as a great land, a 'land of dreams'. The idea that immigrant men would return 'home' was quickly dismissed after the early men experienced the advantages that vilayat could offer them and their families. The decision to emigrate was not an individual decision but a family decision. Many Pakistani immigrants considered Britain as a distant country but one to which they had become linked during the years of colonial and imperial expansion (Holmes, 1991). Attitudes before immigration were quite different, partly based on the British rule in India and partly to do with stereotypes, where the majority of rural Pakistanis considered Britain as a foreign and an alien country. However, when the opportunity arose to come to Britain in search of a better economic and social life such public attitudes became less prominent.

The majority of the early immigrants were employed in jobs which were the most easily available for the newly arrived immigrants, and the jobs that English workers did not want to do. In times of full employment, and the demand for more skilled and highly paid labour, the local indigenous labour force became upwardly mobile by moving into better employment (Rose et al, 1969). It is important to put this in context. Before the arrival of immigrants many of the White working-class population were employed in low status jobs and many continued to do so after the arrival of immigrants. Normal class differences in terms of occupation prevailed.

In order to understand the context of settlement and employment patterns of first migrants it is important to note that, regardless of their caste, the vast majority of Pakistani males began their working life in factories and other manual related employment i.e. restaurants, driving taxis and working on the buses. This bound many Pakistanis together through circumstance and this was to be temporary. The majority of the early immigrants began working in industries which were losing ground in terms of pay and status. Jobs were taken in public transport or those jobs that were considered unpleasant by the host country, like working in the foundries (Modood, 1997). We often overlook the fact that the majority of Pakistani migrants had been used to working in manual labour and had adapted to the same working environment in Britain without too much adjustment. Working alongside fellow kinsmen made the situation easier.

Many studies have pointed out that the early Pakistani immigrants were employed doing 'dirty jobs' such as in the textile industry. This for some was the result of deliberate racism and discrimination. However, most Pakistani men, especially those from the lower castes who worked in the textile industry saw it as something quite different. Of course the work was hard and involved long hours but it was also an opportunity 'too good to miss'. It was a good starting base for future aspirations and opportunities such as buying one's own house, becoming a landlord or becoming self-employed. They were also in a position to support their family and kin members in the United Kingdom and those left back in Pakistan. The early employment allowed for much of this to happen and opportunities were quickly taken up. For most Pakistanis belonging to the lowest castes, getting a job outside of one's caste was practically impossible. High unemployment among the men was a feature for most lower caste families in Pakistan coupled with very low wages. The opportunities in Britain were seen as 'goldmine' by most of these individuals and biraderi.

However, for the well-qualified individuals the situation was often quite different; most had no guarantee that they would obtain employment equivalent to their qualifications (Tomlinson, 1984). A national survey by Smith (1977) found that many Asian men were working in jobs for which they were 'over qualified'. In addition many individuals who were holders of overseas qualifications were often not accepted. The DES for example insisted that teachers trained overseas must re-train in Britain (Tomlinson, 1984). It was estimated that in 1949 there was about one thousand doctors practising in the UK (Kondapi, 1951). Others who had obtained degrees from Pakistan were offered cleaning jobs, which they regarded as being insulting when they wished to do white-collar jobs (Bhatti, 1999). The question remains whether traditional employment trends still have repercussions or whether the position of immigrants has changed since their first arrival in to the United Kingdom.

Sending remittances still remain habits which have been long established and remain standard among many older Pakistanis. Khan (1979) found that the remittances sent to Mirpur improved both the general standard of living and also contributed towards the economy of Mirpur through investment. The early Pakistanis remitted as much as half of their earnings. It was estimated that in 1963 26 million pounds was remitted, which amounted to more than the whole inland revenue of East Pakistan (Khan, 1979; Lewis, 1994). This demonstrates a dependent connection between kin in Britain and those who still remained back in Mirpur. Many large new houses were built in the new Mirpur City with remittances sent by relatives from Britain (Lewis, 1994). This would ensure that close ties with the country of origin would continue (Khan, 1979). Most build houses to show off their wealth to biraderi but also to non-biraderi members. This gave most a sense of satisfaction that 'they had made it' but at the same time, this created resentment and hostility among biraderi members.

Building larger decorative houses or buying land was a common goal for most, even if it meant that they would stay empty or had to find tenants. Wealth had to be shown off for everyone to see. This was not uncommon where whole families immigrated to the United Kingdom. This trend has continued to the present day, where some parents go back to Pakistan to build houses. This trend is likely to decrease as increasing numbers of young people born and raised in Britain view this money as being spent inappropriately. Money remitted was rarely used for other purposes such as investment in education or schooling for those young relatives left behind. Only a small number used remittances to pay for schooling or university fees (a goal for most before migration to the UK). This created dependence rather than encouraging the young to enter a profession or to become self-employed. Some did not want to do anything because they knew of the arrangements made for them to enter the UK at a later date, for marriage purposes.

This influx of capital and investment into Mirpur had important repercussions on the traditional power structure, whereby some tenant peasant farmers became independent landowners who had a continuous supply of capital from Britain. The change for some Pakistanis from being landless to being landowners was dramatic and was felt throughout the wider community. They became the new gentry, the 'upper crust' of the community where Pakistanis would look up to them with respect. Despite or because of the influx of remittances sent to Mirpur, those relatives left behind quickly became aware of the opportunities available in Britain and wanted to become part of that success. British Pakistanis have always been viewed as being affluent by those relatives in Pakistan; a label that continues to prevail.

The significance of acquiring this wealth could be seen within the Pakistani community. The izzat increased in accordance with the newfound wealth. For lower caste families this meant they could purchase land, gain increased access to services such as medical, electricity and water supply and also meant an increase in the prestige of the family. To an extent this new wealth meant an increase in power and authority within one's own biraderi (Raza, 1993). One effect of this was that it created divisions between fellow biraderi members. Lower caste members, with financial resources, attempted to distance themselves from those considered as having less money. This led to fragmented castes/biraderis and the creation of sub-castes/biraderis.

The money sent to Pakistan was used to pay off debts and to support family and relatives. Some early successful Pakistanis living and working in Britain invested large amounts of money in Mirpur. Dahya (1973), for example, found that in the district of Jehlum, Pakistani migrants had built a cinema, petrol station and flats (Khan, 1979). The important issue is to what extent this still has a hold on their sense of duty and their sentimental attachment to Pakistan. Nothing causes a more permanent feeling than dependency. Without doubt regions such as Mirpur have benefited enormously from remittances and the city has become prosperous.

Amongst some families there was a sense of obligation and guilt if individuals did not provide monthly or yearly payments for relatives still left 'back home'. Bhatti (1999) found that individuals who did not follow this rule were seen as a failure and an ungrateful exile. This suggests the tension between the obligation to show loyalty and perhaps resentment towards their own community, i.e. having to send remittances as an obligation. It also says something about the continuing importance of networks of relationships in terms of kinship. The younger generation appears to continue the practice, although not to the same extent, depending on employment and family circumstances.

Remittances continue to play an important part in the link between the 'prosperous' British Pakistanis and those relatives who still depend on remittances. It is important to note that only some relatives have benefited from remittances and only those considered to be part of the family received this money. This is perhaps a stereotype of Pakistanis who sent remittances because it suggests that the 'biraderi looks after its own'. Most did not receive any financial benefit at all. Despite an increase in financial resources for some lower caste families, they still remained in the same caste. This meant that the social status of immigrants, of fellow biraderi, was still being judged by the caste system. This is quite different from the concept of a Western 'social class' system, which was alien to the vast majority of rural immigrants who have been brought up under the caste system.

The biraderi and the sense of belonging

The Pakistani emigration became highly organized and depended upon the system of sponsorship and patronage, which was selective and was confined to certain districts of Pakistan like Mirpur. Later, as the first migrants became more settled in terms of employment and accommodation, they sponsored other kinsmen to these parts (Rose et al, 1969; Ghuman, 1994). There are, after all, parallels between these habits and Western concepts such as 'networking' and nepotism. In many ways the early immigrants moved old traditional habits to Britain. Hospitality, the providing of accommodation and the supporting of kinsmen, was an obligation placed on all early immigrants. This has to be examined within the context of the community that is not just defensive in terms of protecting itself from the wider White community (Allen, 1971).

The lack of immigration control before the Commonwealth Immigration Act of 1962 was to perpetuate the selective process of migration, where kinsmen and fellow villagers already in the UK stood a better chance of sponsoring other kinsmen to enter without Vouchers. This led to a dramatic decline in the number of workers coming to the UK to dependents only and resulted in chain migration (Price, 1969; Deakin, 1970; Anwar 1986; 1998). This was based on primary social relationships with previous migrants (MacDonald and MacDonald, 1962). It entitled the UK passport holder and his close dependants to the right to enter and settle in Great Britain, rather than those individuals who had no kinship ties with Britain (Bhat, 1988; Skellington, 1996). This is an ironic reflection of kinship. However, dependents of legally settled migrants faced difficulties in gaining entry to the UK (CRE, 1985a; CRE, 1989a). Immigration was closely linked with village and kinship networks (Holmes, 1991). Roger Ballard mentioned that, although a large Asian population may reside in a particular city, internally significant communal aggregation often includes no more than one hundred families (Rapoport et al, 1982).

Asian immigrants who came to be joined by their wives and families and by other Asians mostly came from the same region, caste or religion, and later formed communities within their own distinct lifestyles. Family unity, caste network, religious and social cohesion and the belief in mutual help among the early immigrants were all necessary for social stability and economic success (Andrews, 1991). It is argued that mutual support, which is part of Pakistani life, has also led to a ghetto mentality among some Pakistanis. Village-kin networks played an important role in the process of chain migration and district ties were established in Britain. Relatives reinforce arranged marriages operating within these networks by the formation of graveyard networks through committees (Ranger et al, 1996).

The sponsorship by friends and relations in the United Kingdom, on the basis of fellow villagers and kin ties, was a necessary insurance against hardship during the early days of settlement (Anwar, 1998; Allen, 1971). This may have been a deliberate decision made by the Government that new arrivals to the United Kingdom would have a better chance of adapting to a foreign country if fellow biraderi were already settled in the United Kingdom in terms of financial and emotional support. The relationship between kinsmen was essentially an economic one. The majority of Pakistanis settled in towns and cities where there was plenty of opportunity to find work coupled with low-cost accommodation (see R. Ballard, 1994). Travel agents set up offices in Mirpur and played a crucial role in the migration of Pakistanis to the UK dealing with paperwork and other matters. This was particularly important since the vast majority of Pakistanis who arrived in the UK were illiterate (Dahya, 1968). They often helped potential migrants to find a way around restrictions imposed by the Pakistani government who wished to reduce the numbers emigrating (Rose et al, 1969).

Illiteracy was high among the early immigrant men and even higher among the women who arrived later. The majority did not see illiteracy as a barrier to their aspirations because the United Kingdom offered them opportunities. It was hoped future British-born Pakistani children would take advantage and do even better. This is where the biraderi was important because it offered support and laid the foundations for permanency. Future arrivals would fit into the structure and take on their share of responsibilities to help others. Perhaps the most striking example is housing. In a relatively short period of time Pakistanis have moved from rented back-to back accommodation to becoming owner-occupiers to becoming landlords in forty-five years. This is a remarkable achievement given all difficulties faced by the early arrivals and not forgetting the contribution older Pakistanis have made to the British economy.

The first migrants settled together irrespective of origin but as the rate of immigration increased sub-groups developed based on regional identity, which divided into village and kinship units (Rose et al, 1969) and which were also based on caste and religion (Ghuman, 1994). Further divisions appeared based on religious sects i.e. Sunnis, Shias and Ahmadiyya. In Bradford, Rose found that there was little communication between groups of West Pakistanis who had developed extensive family clusters (Rose et al, 1969; Ranger et al, 1996). Their allegiance to specific groups was not immediately apparent but beneath the surface, there are multiple divisions from 'Black/White' to 'Afro/Pakistanis' to 'Indian/Muslims' and indeed among Muslims (or Christians).

Chain migration was the usual pattern. Men would send for their families to join a settled kinsman who would act as their sponsor. They, in turn, would subsequently sponsor other male relatives (Allen, 1971; Lewis, 1994). Werbner (1990), in her study of Pakistanis living in Manchester, showed that, as the numbers of Pakistanis increased, individuals became more selective in choosing their friends who were of the same type of class background, the same region of origin or the same sectarian religious beliefs. In the pioneering days when saving money was the overriding goal, groups of Pakistani men would share the same house. The immediate result was a reduction in rent paid. Individuals had savings to purchase expensive consumer goods, for example televisions, washing machines and cars (Rapoport et al, 1982). The research issue is whether such traditions have continued to influence British-born Pakistanis or whether there has been a shift in generational values.

Communal living was a characteristic of the early immigrants. It provided an insurance policy for fellow countrymen who fell out of work. The early migrants believed that economic goals were more likely to be achieved through mutual support than through dispersal into the wider community, and this helped keep migrants' families together (Hiro, 1991; Lewis, 1994). This connects, of course, the concept of nepotism or networking; the support of one's own culture in the face of outsiders, whatever the moral basis.

Communal living also ensured conformity to traditional norms and the avoidance of contacts outside the immediate sub-group, apart from visiting the homes of fellow kinsmen. Early settlers relied on their kin to help them achieve their economic goals but also in other ways, such as helping each other in times of illness and crisis and greeting new arrivals into the United Kingdom (Rose et al, 1969). Joint communal living and group activities for most Pakistani men also meant a total lack of privacy in the house. On the surface this suggests that communal living was a basis for a common goal among the early immigrants, whether this was economic or emotional attachment, but does not take into account any disputes that may have arisen between individuals. It is argued that communal living was a necessity rather than the preferred choice, especially when this meant sharing a house with individuals from different castes and religious sects. As soon as Pakistanis could afford their accommodation they moved out of communal living. This was an early indication of how the stereotypical 'close-knit biraderi' would fragment after only a short while in the UK.

As the early years of settlement elapsed, Pakistani-owned shops began to serve their own community because White shops did not stock 'Asian foods'; nor could they cater for diverse and ethnic tastes. This was an opportunity to quickly develop business and enterprise that would help to create Asian/Pakistani entrepreneurs who took (often with the help of the biraderi or family) the opportunity by selling anything from lentils to halal meat; from chapatti flour to spices. This was made possible by a continued and sustained infrastructure of importers, wholesalers and retailers. As this took hold some successful Pakistanis went into manufacturing. Much of this was made possible by the strong links in Pakistan who could supply goods and materials at the desired price and quality. Bradford was typical of most towns and cities which had a sizeable Pakistani population. For example in 1967, there were 51 Pakistani greengrocers and butchers shops compared with two in 1959. There were also 50 Pakistani-owned Schools of Motoring; the number of cafes rose from three in 1959 to 16 in 1967; the number of barbers rose from three to 16 and there were five Pakistani banks in Bradford. Other Pakistani-owned businesses included travel agencies and dry cleaners. The situation was similar in other parts of Britain such as Balsall Heath and Glasgow (Rose et al, 1969; Lewis, 1994). In 1965, 105 immigrants owned commercial and business premises in Bradford (Hiro, 1991). This growth was replicated in other towns such as Glasgow, which at that time had a Pakistani population of 7,000 and had one hundred retail grocers and 25 wholesale stores (Elahi, 1967). This was a demonstration of the commitment of early Pakistanis to succeed in the UK.

On a different issue an early study by Dahya (1965) found that young male immigrants were as secular as their contemporaries in British society. Dahya found little religious observance on the part of early migrants; few attended the mosque for prayers, and Pakistani-owned cafes remained open during the month of Ramzan. However, the arrival of wives and children changed much of this early practice, and women regularly prayed and transmitted religious beliefs and values to their children. This suggests that early immigrants had adapted to the host culture free of constraints from biraderi pressures.

Life for the majority of young Pakistanis became home-centred. Visits to the pub declined as men began spending most of their leisure time improving the house. Spare money was saved to purchase items such as furniture, television or a car (Hiro, 1991; Lewis, 1994). It could be argued that close kinship ties in terms of leisure activities could act as a cultural stranglehold by parents and elders over the actions of young people. However, Asian women who joined their husbands were not totally immune to environmental influence. Most Pakistani women discarded the veil. By contrast, a firm line was taken in the case of their daughters, with the insistence that they must dress modestly and remain chaste before marriage. Such beliefs were based on the majority of Asian immigrants who considered British society as morally decadent (Hiro, 1991). The important issue is whether traditional practices, especially by older Pakistani males, remain significant, i.e. whether religious observance or habits have changed over time.

In some quarters it was expected that the first migrants who came to Britain would eventually cut themselves off from the culture and adapt to the British way of life (Stopes-Roe and Cochrane, 1990). This oversimplified the view that the first immigrants would quickly discard their existing traditions and values and take on British ones. Many Muslim communities in Britain have been very successful in reproducing much of their traditional social and cultural world. In addition, in Muslim areas, individuals live in self-contained communities where they are in a position to sustain an institutional and economic infrastructure that embodies religious and cultural norms (Lewis, 1994). All groups of immigrants who come to a foreign country have enormous difficulties in adjusting to a new way of life. The first wave of Asian people arriving in Britain faced severe problems, which were related to differences in religion, language and custom. Thus, the majority of Asian people turned to their own community for protection and understanding (Anwar, 1976).

There are still signs of this, especially among older Pakistanis. An example of this is the enormous number of services and goods offered to fellow countrymen. To those outside the community there appears to be an understanding between individuals. Beneath the surface there is tension within the biraderi members and also between groups, based on caste and religious sect. Particular families are obliged to help each other, and to unfairly discriminate against others. In positions of influence or power this led to corruption.

Migration has always been a controversial issue both socially and politically. During periods of mass migration to the UK White and non-White immigrants faced hostility when looking for employment and housing (Engels, 1952). *The Royal Commission on Population* (1949) suggested it would be more difficult in terms of integrating non-White immigrants into the wider society (Political and Economic Planning, 1948) and led to calls to control migration (The Cabinet Papers, 1950). This cause was taken up by Members of Parliament during the 1964 General Election and Peter Griffiths of the Conservative Party ran an anti-immigration campaign and defeated the Labour Shadow Foreign Secretary in Smethwick (Hartley-Brewer, 1965). Although defeated at the 1966 General Election he returned to Parliament in 1979 as the member for Portsmouth North (Layton-Henry, 1992). Perhaps the most famous of all was Enoch Powell, Member of Parliament for Wolverhampton South West, who made speeches against large-scale migration and his 'rivers of blood' speech on 20 April 1968 (Cosgrave, 1990). Rising anti-immigration sentiment led to the formation of the British National Party who contested elections in the 1970s. Another party was the British Campaign to Stop Immigration (BCSI) who contested in the 1972 Parliamentary by-elections (Anwar, 1973; 1974; 1975).

The more recent arrivals of asylum seekers have reignited the debate on minority ethnic communities in the UK. According to some, race relations between the majority White and minority ethnic groups are at crisis point, and community cohesion appears to take centre stage for policy makers. The central question is how to integrate all communities. Some have adapted to the British way of life, for example, British-born Pakistanis or British-born Indians, while the new asylum seekers (like all new immigrants) will need a process of adjustment. This process will not only depend on the White majority but also on the existing minority ethnic groups in the United Kingdom in terms how of quickly they can settle and integrate.

Family life

The village household is often three generational, comprising of grandparent(s), married son(s), their wives(s) and children and unmarried son(s) and daughter(s). Property is communally owned whether the source of this is through work, land or wage labour, and decisions are communally made. The final decision rests with the head of the family, the eldest male, and authority is allocated according to gender and age (Khan, 1979). It is important to bear in mind that the izzat of the family is crucial for parents and biraderi elders.

Beyond the household there are biraderi members (kin groups) whose members claim descent in a paternal line from a common male ancestor. Raza (1993) argued that in village society the individual forms part of a complex network of rights and obligations, which extend outwards from his/her immediate family to that of kin and fellow villagers. He defined biraderi as, 'it includes all men who can trace their relationship to a common ancestor, no matter how remote. The descent group biraderi includes all these who claim and can trace links of a common paternal link'. Within the Pakistani community, biraderi elders have considerable power and are respected figures and have the power to reprimand deviants, thus maintaining the izzat of the group (Khan, 1979).

Individualism and independence so revered by the West appears selfish to Pakistanis, who expect and value dependency and loyalty to kin members and kin groups. Within the Pakistani family individual rights are dictated by age, sex and the order of birth. One of the main characteristics of village life is that everyone knows each other: close friends are classified as 'brothers' and 'sisters'. This network of friends and family also ensures conformity and deviants are 'pulled back' into line by the community (Khan, 1979; Rapoport et al, 1982). The family is the vehicle for conveying the group norms to ensure its survival sustained by a religious ethos, and it is the religious element that gives these norms the strength and enforces the values of the biraderi (Basit, 1997). Individualism fostered by the White culture is almost unknown to people from rural Pakistan, who work and live together and where individuals are expected to be loyal and respectful to fellow kin members. In cases of disobedience, social pressure is exercised on its members to conform to traditional values (Hiro, 1991). One possible outcome of this process may be that it has led to a clash in outlook within the community where those with influence show favouritism to certain relatives.

There are enormous pressures to conform to the norms of the community. The community treated deviants harshly. For example, unmarried girls who did not fulfil the expected role of marriage and childbearing were controlled by force, since this not only affects the girl's reputation but also her family and kin groups as well. These clear-cut rules about rights and obligations of family members contribute to a certain amount of stability (Khan, 1979). It is important to take into account that the close-knit communal structure can be a cause of conflict within the family and the wider Pakistani community. There is also a stereotypical assumption that elders resolve any tension that exists between young people and parents but this fails to see that young people are challenging the very authority of their parents and elders. It is important to place Khan in the context of her time, since many people still assume that nothing has changed. To understand the present it is necessary to acknowledge the context of the past, but not to assume that nothing has changed.

In terms of biraderi relations, Raza argued that the individual does not act on his own behalf but his/her reputation depends upon theirs and the fulfilling of obligations ascribed to him, which as a result keeps the family 'bound' together (Raza, 1993).

Leonard and Speakman (1986) also found that in parts of the UK, for example Wales, and in certain ethnic groups including South Asians and Cypriots, who stress family relationships and recognize obligations to kin beyond the nuclear family more than some other communities (Basit, 1997). Wilson (1978) defined izzat as 'the sensitive and many faceted male identity which can change as the situation demands it – from family honour to self-respect and sometimes to pure male ego' (in Adams, 1978). Ballard argued that in its narrow sense 'izzat' is a matter of male pride (Rapoport et al, 1982). Izzat has different meanings depending on the context and varies for example, 'honour', 'status', 'respect', 'obedience' and 'loyalty'.

Family members are expected to be loyal to the family, where they are expected to show obedience to elders. However, Farrukh Hashmi found that there were some early cases of young Pakistanis who rejected their community, and were condemned by fellow kinsmen. The cost to the individual in breaking with tradition was high. The individual lost the support of his fellow immigrants. This was coupled with the difficulty of living alone in an alien country (Allen, 1971). In this context condemnation is no light matter, and can lead to exacting revenge.

Similarly, Roger Ballard argued that most parents put a great deal of effort into ensuring that they transmit the basic tenets of family morality to their children. The need to put loyalty before self-interest is constantly stressed to young people. Ballard showed that some parents blackmail their children in order to exercise control. The loss of izzat; the family would suffer if any one of their children should depart too much from established norms, is taken very seriously (Rapoport et al, 1982).

Early experience of Pakistani women

What distinguished Pakistani emigration from any other emigration in the early period was the imbalance between the sexes (Miles, 1993). This imbalance was to do with cultural patterns of the Muslim community and the seclusion and the subordination of women within the Pakistani household. For cultural reasons women remained in Pakistan under the protection of other family males rather than expose them to a foreign and an alien land (Rose et al, 1969; Ghuman, 1994).

The early experience of Pakistani women was one of isolation. The Pakistani women, who arrived in the United Kingdom, experienced extreme loneliness and were unable to leave the house without their husbands. Pakistani women were not only restricted by the practice of purdah but also by their lack of English skills (Rose et al, 1969). Khan (1979) found that on the arrival of Pakistani women into Britain, they reinforced the Muslim culture, where they kept in strict purdah and were isolated from the local indigenous population. This was to protect women from Western influences and bolster traditionally held beliefs.

The arrival of immigrant women and children meant the strict segregation of activities between males and females within the Pakistani household and that male members worked and spent their leisure in the company of other men (Allen, 1971). The experiences of rural women differed from those of middle-class women: where many women from prosperous backgrounds, i.e. Islamabad and Karachi, enjoy such freedoms as working, attending university and participating in leisure activities, the lifestyles of these women are in stark contrast to the lives of rural Pakistani women. There are complex inheritances that remain significant in the present day and the consequences can still be seen.

Certain factors forced early immigrant women to find work. This meant a change in living habits from joint living to a smaller nuclear family. Secondly, there was always pressure to increase the family's income. There is also evidence of an increasing number of Asian women working in factories in places such as in parts of Southall and Slough who subsidize the family's income (Hiro, 1991). Emphasizing the gender differences in cultural practices, Rose et al (1969) noted that the female is considered as a debt to the family (Rose et al, 1969; Rapoport et al, 1982). This attitude has always been dominant among Pakistani Muslims. Similarly, Raza (1993) argued that Pakistani women are considered as a liability, but sometimes are treated as 'assets' for economic reasons. For example, a marriage into a more affluent family can bring investment and inheritance for the girls' family. In Raza's Islamic opinion it is important to distinguish between the attitudes of the Muslim community and Islam, where the position of women is the result of the patriarchal society the Pakistanis originated.

Role of parents and elders

Certain traditional habits have been long established. An example is the extended Pakistani family which rests on the concept of primogeniture, where authority is vested in the father, upon whose death the authority is passed down to the eldest son. Maintaining the traditional hierarchy of authority within the family is essential for them, but there are some young Pakistanis who maintain public authority and respect due to elders, whilst others may question or disobey their elders. Khan argued that on some occasions Pakistani parents placed the blame on the influence of British education on their children as a source of tension between British-born youngsters and their parents (Khan, 1979). Roger Ballard argued that as the age of the father increases he only retains a symbolic authority but is reassured by formal respect, which the sons are usually prepared to offer. He argued that sons are aware that it is only through their fathers that they can gain access to land and retain their good name in their community (Rapoport et al, 1982).

The traditional leadership and authority for the majority of working class Pakistanis in Britain comes from the Ulama. The majority of Imams come from the Sub-Continent, from small villages and biraderis so that individual loyalties lie with specific groups. As a result of a lack of basic knowledge of Islam, many of the teachings of Islam are based on demeaning the doctrines of other religious sects, i.e. Sunnis, Shias and other groups, which inevitably results in differences (Raza, 1993).

Caste

In order to understand this community it is important to explain their belief in the caste system. Before the independence of Pakistan from India in 1947, Muslims, Hindus and Sikhs lived together in towns and villages across India, although each of these communities had their own traditions, norms and beliefs. Over a period of time some of the traits of Hinduism and Sikhism became fused into the culture of Pakistanis/Muslims. This fusion between the Hindu and the Pakistani culture can be seen from examining marriage rituals and the practice of dowry. In Hinduism, the family of the bride must give a dowry to the groom, which can include a combination of money, gold and land (especially in Pakistan).

Singh (1959) found that before the separation of Pakistan, Muslims, Sikhs and Hindus commonly visited one another's shrines and that many Muslim holy men had Hindu followers (Taylor, 1976). Caste plays an important part in the lives of Hindus, which determines the life chances of every individual. The highest caste in Hinduism is Brahman (Pardesh, 1994). Men born in this caste become priests and scholars and provide the spiritual leadership of their community. At the bottom of the caste hierarchy, and deprived of caste affiliation, are the outcasts who are labelled as engaging in demeaning or polluting occupations by the society. The origins of the caste system can be dated as far back as 1500 BC to the ancient sacred writing of Rig-Veda (Skjonsberg, 1982).

Social stratification in Pakistan is based on the caste system. Unlike the Hindu system the Pakistani caste system is not religiously based but cultural. The highest caste in Pakistan is the Rajah or Jats, who are the landed gentry, the traditional ruling class in Pakistan. The lowest castes are Kamini, landless labourers, for example the Majaar caste, i.e. shoesmith, blacksmith (Ranger et al, 1996). The social structure of the villages from which migrants are drawn closely parallels that of a Hindu caste system made up of a number of largely endogamous and nominally occupationally linked descent groups (Shaw, 1994). The majority of those who emigrated to the United Kingdom belonged to the lowest castes, i.e. shoesmith, blacksmith or the Majaar caste (landless group), who were economically and socially deprived in Mirpur/Pakistan. The common view held that there was little incentive for such groups to remain in Pakistan and they saw the opportunity to better themselves by coming to Britain (Khan, 1979).

By contrast, there was little to encourage high caste members to migrate to Britain. Their position in Pakistan is secure and many of them live in relative comfort. However, a small number of high caste individuals did migrate to Britain. These groups remain segregated from the wider Pakistani community, creating an elite of their own. The majority of high caste members were more ambitious and, with more resources, purchased businesses with the help of family and fellow caste members. This appears to be the standard habit among such individuals. Again this has parallels with economics and nepotism and the acknowledgement of work with fellow kin members to achieve economic goals.

Shaw (1994), in her study of Pakistanis living in Oxford, found that those who became prosperous in Oxford are by no means always from high-caste families, or those who had a dominant position in the village hierarchy. In a highly industrialized country like Britain the socio-economic position of the individual is associated with social class, which is more open and allows mobility. Where a lower caste individual or family has acquired wealth or entered professions such as medicine or law, it is not uncommon for individuals to adapt or change their family name to more socially acceptable ones such as Chowdery, Malik or Bhatti. It is argued that lower caste members adjusted better to the British environment because the social system in the West is based on 'class' as opposed to a caste system, which meant that opportunities in accessing education and employment in Pakistan were very limited. Although they suffered from racial discrimination in the UK this was not viewed as being worse than the prejudice they suffered at home.

Summary

The Pakistanis who came to the UK were economic migrants in search of their dream. The majority of those arriving in the UK belonged to the lower castes and many those had little opportunity to better themselves back in Pakistan. England was vilayat, 'a place of dreams'. The early immigrants had a purpose and a goal, to better themselves and provide a base for their children who would have many more opportunities available to them.

Belonging to a lower caste prepared them for most eventualities and the difficulties they would face such as discrimination and poor housing. The vast majority of Pakistanis adjusted well to the British environment given the early hardships endured. Very few of the early arrivals returned to Pakistan permanently. The early impact of settlement was cushioned upon the arrival of family and relatives; this allowed for extended family and biraderi support to be developed and kinship ties were strengthened. Increased financial resources and biraderi support meant that most Pakistanis could afford to buy their own house much earlier. The purchase of property led to most Pakistanis settling among their own biraderi members, often along the lines of caste and sect. This would result in self-imposed segregated communities within the larger heading of the 'Pakistani community'. Importantly this appears to be largely out of choice rather than imposed.

The continued connection with 'home' remains strong, particularly among the first immigrants, for example in terms of sending remittances, contact with relatives and the building of family homes. For the vast majority of older Pakistanis this is and will remain only a sentimental attachment to 'home' (Pakistan). It is understandable that they have maintained links with Pakistan. The question is whether the next generation will adhere to this.

Chapter 4

From Manningham to Burnley to Oldham: What Should We Learn?

Background to the disturbances and the reports

There is a tendency that when any major disturbances (or riots) occur some common issues come to light: distrust of the police, high unemployment, poor education and poor housing are identified as 'triggers'. A good illustration is the *Bradford Commission report*, which examined some of the causes of the disturbances in Manningham, Bradford during the summer of 1995. It acknowledged that poor education, overcrowded homes, poverty and unemployment pressures, which are prominent among the young ethnic minority population, act as a predisposition to tensions and violence (*Bradford Commission Report*, 1996).

These have been the focus of all inquiries and the subsequent reports from Manningham to Burnley to Oldham. Some argue that the common link in all the disturbances is the underlying issues of race and racism suffered by minority ethnic groups in the UK. This is the focus of so much debate that it distracts us from understanding the underlying issues common to all communities. There is also a problem with terminology in describing what occurred and whether these were disturbances, riots or race riots. The disturbances should highlight the general concerns among all young people. The causes and the effects of exclusion from the wider society are acknowledged, but often overlooked is the exclusion people suffer within their own communities. As a result the wrong issues are sometimes highlighted, such as racism, segregation or strained community (race) relations.

The disturbances in Manningham, Bradford during the summer of 1995 were followed by further disturbances in 2001 and also in Burnley and Oldham. Several major local and national reports were published that shed some light on the 'causes' of the disturbances. The problem with official reports is that they have a tendency to be ignored and are often treated with suspicion when important messages can be overlooked or, at worst, dismissed outright. Another reason for dismissing the conclusions was the strong feeling within the community that all Pakistanis were labelled as criminal or prone to anti-establishment violence and reaction. Regardless of the relatively small number of young Pakistani men who were involved in the disturbances the 'label stuck' to the whole community. The vast majority of Pakistanis (both young and old) did not condone the behaviour of the minority whatever the underlying issues.

Riots or disturbances are not uncommon on the UK mainland. The disturbances in Toxteth and Brixton in the 1980s caused untold damage to the Black community, which, to an extent, is still trying to repair the damage. Towns and cities affected remain synonymous with the disturbances and once a community is stigmatized, with all the wrong labels, it becomes nearly impossible to 'get rid of'. This has a psychological effect on the residents and not just those directly involved. What is clear is that the actions of the few in Bradford have affected all communities who reside within the district. The disturbances have had a 'rippling effect' on community relations, while in some places they have become almost invisible. The 2001 disturbances were different. Some argued that all 'Asians' were grouped together, i.e. Indian and Bangladeshi, and created a sense of alienation with a backdrop of immigration of asylum seekers, the Gulf War and 9/11. The disturbances raised issues of the integration of Asian minority communities into the British culture, while for others the disturbances raised questions of racism and deprivation.

For some the disturbances became a time of reflection to see what they could do, as individuals and as part of communities, to restore harmony and trust between communities (and also within the community). It was also a wake-up call for both the minority and majority communities. The elders were seen to play a crucial role in the process of building harmony and trust between the various communities. They can work in partnership with parents and young people to discuss issues of concern, and to work with the police and other agencies on ways to build bridges. There has to be real dialogue and at the same time, the young people have to be an integral part of this dialogue process.

Although the disturbances were the work of a minority of young people, they highlighted wider discontent with their own communities and with the pressures faced from wider society common to most young people. At the same time they tarnished the name of the majority of Pakistanis who are law-abiding citizens. What was new about these disturbances is that those primarily involved were 'Asian' or 'Pakistani', often considered passive by most people. These disturbances were different because previously we had seen disturbances in Notting Hill, Toxteth and Brixton and those involved were mainly young men from the Black/Afro-Caribbean communities. According to some the underlying issues were similar, including the distrust of the police. The disturbances were also a 'wake-up' call to institutions and organizations that have contact with minority ethnic communities (and also with the White communities) that something needed to be done.

It is also important to remember the context of the reports. The inquiry came about because of these particular disturbances. It is arguable there should have been, and still needs to be, a comprehensive study of 'Pakistanis', more specifically the relationship between young Pakistanis and their parents within the community in Bradford rather than focusing purely on the disturbances. The reports have two tasks to consider after the disturbances: the immediate and the contextual. It is argued here that the examinations focused on the event rather than explaining the context of the event. Some of the flaws of the reports are obvious. The reports accept too many views of older people and institutions (the ones accused of being 'institutionally racist') without allowing for the views of more young people, and in particular the marginalized groups such as females, to make comment and to have their say as well as the ordinary members of the communities. The context of the reports should be examined within the boundaries of political considerations, expediency and time.

Bradford disturbances

Manningham is a culturally and ethnically diverse area, unlike some other parts of Bradford where, albeit in small pockets, one group may be in the majority. Manningham has been the home to several minority ethnic groups, including a large Pakistani and Bangladeshi population as well Black/Caribbean, White and more recently home to asylum seekers. For some this can create problems, while for others social and economic problems associated with Manningham, such as inadequate housing, lack of suitable employment and crime, are major issues.

Statistics show that in the Toller district (where the disturbances took place) 39.3 per cent of the population is employed compared to the English average of 60.6 per cent, but it has a higher number of those unemployed compared to the English average (7 per cent and 3.4 per cent respectively) or even when compared to the Bradford average of 4.4 per cent. Its residents are also more likely to have 'no qualifications' compared to the English average (45.5 per cent and 29.1 per cent respectively) or even when compared to the Bradford average of 35.1 per cent (National Census, 2001). All of these were seen as the backdrop to the disturbances.

The first in a series of reports was the *Bradford Commission report* (1996), which examined the disturbances in the summer of 1995 in Manningham, Bradford. The Terms of Reference of the inquiry were: 'to conduct hearings to consider the wider implications for Bradford of recent events in a part of the inner city of Bradford, in order to help create a better future for all people of the district and to promote peace, harmony and understanding between the communities of Bradford' (*Bradford Commission report*, 1996). The *Bradford Commission report* had two major themes and arguments. The first is the part played by both the police and the local Pakistani/ Asian community before and during the disturbances and the 'arrests', which took place on the 9th of June. The second theme was the broadening of the inquiry, the examination of the Pakistani community in areas such as: arranged marriages; the role of young women; education; employment; drugs and crime.

The Commission concluded the disturbances were the consequences of tensions and disorder that are present in many parts of Bradford. The Commission found that the direct cause of the disorders was the 'unacceptable behaviour of those relatively few people who behaved so anti-socially" (*Bradford Commission report*, 1996). The Commission rejected any claims as 'superficial', that the disorders occurred because of police racism. Although the Commission did highlight that too many people experienced racism from the police, the Commission did not arrive at this conclusion (*Bradford Commission report*, 1996). The Commission also rejected any notion that the majority of young men in the Muslim community have rejected the values of their parents and any claims that Asian parents have 'lost control' of young people. It highlighted the issue of intergenerational conflict between parents and young people but it left the issue without exploring it in depth.

As the Pakistani community moves away from a minority ethnic community to the fourth generation of British-born young people who have a different understanding of the UK to their 'immigrant' parents, this is a key area where tension is possible. One cause of the disturbances is the ignorance about the Bradford's population. Some suggest that this is a difficult period of the transition process of different communities learning to live together (*Bradford Commission report*, 1996). This is not just a 'race issue' but of all communities (irrespective of race) living together. The important role of institutions was one area of concern to the Commission, it concluded, 'to us, the evidence pointed inescapably to an institutional incapacity to understand, and to relate to, other cultural groupings than the traditional White culture, and in particular to the local Kashmiri community' (*Bradford Commission report*, 1996). Some blame or criticism was being placed on both the community and on institutions.

Others point to conflict within the Pakistani community (which is typical of all) based on generational differences between the young and parents/elders. This is quite different from the 'us' and 'them' attitudes that characterizes simplistic constructions of racial identity. What the report reveals, inadvertently, is as interesting and telling as the conclusions on which the report is based. The conclusions have attracted all the attention and distracted from an analysis of what the evidence reveals. The existence of conflict within the Pakistani community, according to the Bradford Commission, was based upon the generation gap between young Pakistanis and old. However, many of the claims made by the Bradford Commission were not supported by empirical evidence but through general comments made by the public. There was also more evidence available than acknowledged. It appears that the Bradford Commission was on the right track in pursuing this line of enquiry but did not follow this up sufficiently to uncover some of the other causes for the disturbances. There were a number of concerns of young people, including the extent of control held by parents and elders over young people, which played a significant part in the resulting disturbances. The pressure is placed on young people to fulfil their traditional role. This can also affect young people from other communities too. This suggests a tension between the ostensible control exercised by elders and the actual hold on the imagination of young people.

'Control' is favoured as a symbol of social order; the imposition of will over tempestuous youth, 'control' is attractive whilst all parents know control and over-authoritarianism is resisted. There are indications of a battle for 'control' over the cultural meaning given to young people's lives and this battle is significant and possibly unusual. The *Bradford Commission report*, however, accepts the point of view of the older generation without question. It is a somewhat dated, even naive assumption that the older generation have some form of control over the thoughts and actions of their offspring. The opinion is that the older generation of Pakistanis blames their young and the intention of the parents/elders is to control them. For some there was a general failure in the reports to accept the possibility that anti-social behaviour of young people was the result of a deep-rooted and fundamental problem that exists within this community as in any community. Instead, the elders of the community were assumed to have the right to impose their religious and cultural will on the younger generation, and the younger generation should accept this hegenomic position without question.

2001 disturbances

Six years later the UK was to witness more disturbances which appear to be more widespread and damaging to the communities involved and to race relations. These were different from the 1995 disturbances because, on this occasion, the trouble appears on the surface to have started between 'Asian' and White youths. This had racial overtones. Bradford was again at the centre of controversy during 2001. Photographic images were projected across the world as youths clashed with the police who appeared to be under-strength and unprepared for this kind of disturbance on the UK mainland. Most people both within and outside the city were shocked at the events. All of which created a tense atmosphere for the law-abiding residents. The disturbances (unlike in 1995) were not only confined to Bradford but more widespread: Burnley and Oldham were also victims of the disturbances.

This led to a further four reports into the disturbances; two of these were local and two were national in their scope. Institutions were at the centre of investigation about the importance of their role in the community. The Burnley Task Force, chaired by Lord Tony Clarke, was set up after the disturbances in Burnley and gathered evidence from a wide range of local, voluntary and statutory sector representatives. Police were often seen as being soft on drug dealers and unable to deal with other social problems.

The *Oldham Independent Review* had a similar tone, chaired by David Ritchie, although members were drawn from the national stage. The Local Authority and the Police Authority commissioned the research. Again policing is seen as being central in the community and the important role it has to play in community relations was highlighted. This was underlined in the opening paragraph "The police do not create the environment in which they work, but need to influence it, reflect it and respond to its problems" (*Oldham Independent Review*, 2001). The 'Asian' community, both old and young, come across as holding negative views of the police; the role of the police in creating and maintaining segregation was dismissed. The Oldham review points to segregation as predetermined for the social unrest in the town and the local authority plays a major part in this (Kalra, 2002).

Segregation was also a major focus of the two national reports, *Community Cohesion* and *Building Cohesive Communities* (chaired by Ted Cantle), which included inquiries into Bradford, Burnley and Oldham and other towns with minority ethnic populations that did not suffer from social unrest. This marked a change from the two local reports and placed the police at the forefront in creating community cohesion. The criminalization of Black and minority ethnic populations through off-limit areas and drugs were important issues where change needed to occur.

The *Denham report* (led by the Home Office minister, John Denham) focused on the failure of the police, when dealing with communities in these towns, as a concern which allows "weaknesses and disparity in the police response to community issue" (Denham, 2001; see also Kalra, 2002). Although the reports raise important questions they left some issues without examining them in depth. Indeed a broader examination would have shown that the concerns of many Pakistanis are similar to those from the White majority groups. These examinations reveal both the limitations of the original reports, and the reasons behind the limitations. They also offer further insights both into the context of the report and explore in greater depth the underlying internal contradictions in the findings.

'Segregated communities': racism or choice?

A common theme that comes out of the reports is the concept of 'segregated communities' brought to the public attention by Herman Ouseley who chaired the *Community Pride Not Prejudice* (*Ouseley report*, 2001). The report looked at community relations in Bradford. The term is taken to assume that White and minority ethnic groups are geographically segregated from each other and this has a 'knock on' effect on other areas of social and economic life, for example educational segregation (Kalra, 2002). Central to this argument is that racism plays a major part in this process of segregation of different communities. There is too much focus on Asians being segregated from Whites, rather than the other way round (Amin, 2002). Others argue that, as a result of racism, most Asians live in their own areas and White people seek to leave such areas (Kundnani, 2001). The problem with the concept is that communities are marked out in a crude way, highlighting differences where often they do not exist. It attaches blame not only on institutions, which are in a position to respond, but also on individuals.

Some research points to geographical and racial segregation in parts of England such as in Bradford. Visible separation based on colour is a crude way of measuring 'segregation'. This is a simplistic explanation of a complex picture of how individuals and families make choices, or indeed where they choose to live. For others socio-economic factors play a crucial part given the high cost of housing at present. Even if financial resources were available some Pakistanis will continue to live in what are considered to be 'poor areas' because of their loyalty to family and biraderi members. This is not to overlook that there are others who wish to move out if they had the opportunity.

Segregation is often taken to mean racism. For many segregation means that White people deliberately segregate themselves (what is commonly called the 'White flight') from Black and minority ethnic people. The important question is whether this is self-imposed or is a result of deliberate racial segregation. Some members do not want to have any contact with people from different cultures for all sorts of reasons but this could also apply to 'Asian' as well as White people. Segregation can take place for example, among the 'Asian communities', where some Pakistanis and Indians express the desire to live near their own members, and in their own clusters rather than among other 'Asians'. They choose to live near family or friends. There are also differences within communities, which are often overlooked, for example those that exist within communities, those based on sect and caste. Most members would never think of moving elsewhere and away from family and relatives or even form friendships with non-caste/sect members. These are all forms of preferences or forms of deliberate segregation.

On another level, there is also a desire among some Pakistanis who wish to move out of typically 'Pakistani areas'. This is a form of 'Pakistani flight'. In parts of Bradford we can see that as Pakistani families become more prosperous they are moving out into the once considered affluent suburbs of Bradford. This trend is set to continue with the next generation. This can also apply to the 'White community', for example some individuals from the White/English community may choose to live away from areas that have a high number of White/Scottish or White/Welsh residents. The problem is that race is typically used to explain all differences.

Divisions 'within' communities can be just as difficult to overcome as those that exist between communities. The *Bradford Commission report* (1996) concluded that the major obstacle to the commitment of children from ethnic minorities in Bradford is the lack of acknowledgment they receive from the majority of the population, "leading to an unfair and unequal citizenship". This should not overlook the experience of other young people like those from the White/English community who may echo a similar point. Individuals and communities can be marginalized in different ways. There is an enormous amount of research that suggests that young people are marginalized from the wider society that prevents them from participating in education and employment. If minority ethnic communities do not feel part of the community then what will happen with the more recent arrival of asylum seekers or people from the newer countries that have joined the European Union?

Institutional racism

Perhaps the most debated term to be introduced in recent times is 'institutional racism'. The term had originated from the Black Power Movement in the United States. It signifies that institutional procedures, whatever their original purpose, end up discriminating against and disadvantaging Black and other ethnic minorities (Donald and Rattansi, 1992). The term is used in a number of ways, some of which suggest intention, and some of which see manifestations of institutional racism in patterns of disadvantage which affect people who are not White (Mason, 1995).

In the British sense, most people heard of 'institutional racism' after comments made by Sir Paul Condon, the Chief Constable of the Metropolitan Police, to the *MacPherson Inquiry*, relating to the death of the Black teenager, Stephen Lawrence. Most people assumed that the police force is institutionally racist.

The *Bradford Commission report* evidence shows there is an "institutional incapacity" and is not only confined to the police. It concluded that policing in Manningham is "fundamentally flawed" and the two police officers involved were the consequences of that "fundamental flaw". It found that tensions between young people and the police are apparent, and many young local people consider the police as unfair and racist. The Commission concluded that there are some racist police officers in the police force but the Commission did not regard police officers in general as "racist" (*Bradford Commission report*, 1996). It would assume that everyday dealing with the public, every arrest and every investigation could be construed as having racial overtones. The problem is that institutions have been for so long labelled as 'racist' that the label has stuck. It is as if there is a deliberate attempt to make them the targets for attack, as if 'institutional racism' were a matter of policy rather than inadvertent attitudes. This raises the question of what is deliberate and what is inadvertent. 'Intentionality' is a problematic term, in the discussion of bullies and victims, since one can make a typology of bullies but this does not take into account the feelings of the victims and the sometimes accidental nature of hurt. It is when these feelings of victimization are turned round into an argument that there must be some intent that prejudice and discrimination are assumed to be 'institutional'.

The reports into the disturbances attempt to lay the responsibility for the disturbances on particular groups, whether part of a community or part of an institution. This raises another question about the nature of racism. As in the case of feminism it has been argued that discriminatory attitudes go so deep that they are embedded in the very institutions themselves, that they pervade structures as well as agencies. The problem with such arguments is that they cannot easily be disproved, and can be used deliberately to divert attention away from acts of deliberate personal prejudice. On the other hand the way in which an organization can be imbued with its own 'ethos', including pervasive attitudes, is more plausible. It is a term used too often for comfort, and subject to too little research. This is not to suggest that institutions can shed their responsibility, but there are traditional and slow changing institutions that need to adapt to the present climate.

What is overlooked is that racism with all its evils is based on individual prejudice. This is more than just individual preference for, or the dislike of, somebody whether it is based on race, religion or gender. It is like bullying, where the child is picked out for ridicule for being 'different'; for wearing spectacles, or having a different accent maybe; or even whose clothes are somehow made out to be different. 'Different' is the basis for being 'picked on'. Individual prejudice is much more personal. For some institutional racism is to blame, where the structure is at fault; it discriminates deliberately and picks out individuals or communities. This somehow passes the buck onto the institution where individuals can almost be excused for their behaviour. Individuals can almost hide behind the institution and it is still an individual failing.

The concept supposes that institutions systematically disadvantage only Black or Asian groups, but there are other groups, like the White majority, who may at times argue the same. The issue is not simply about 'race', where Black and minority ethnic communities believe they have been disadvantaged. There are also positive outcomes where extra funding can be allocated to groups. For years people have talked about the 'Establishment'. Only more recently has such a term been questioned and subject to change and adaptation. Some groups feel disadvantaged by the traditional structures of society. White/English people for example who live in 'sink estates' have also argued that they are sometimes disadvantaged when financial resources are allocated. They too are concerned, like the minority communities, about their children's education, employment and housing conditions. This creates a sense of injustice that some minority ethnic communities have a political voice but at the same time the needs of White disadvantaged groups can be overlooked or at worse ignored.

Summary

The many reports into the disturbances glimpsed some of the difficulties in the Pakistani community and the complex nature of the 'Pakistani' community, due to the political circumstances. The reports also inadvertently reveal what needs to be explored further, for example segregated communities. On one level the reports reveal distinctions of point of view, for example between the police and other points of view, where the police are viewed as racist. On another level the reports revealed 'conflicts' within the Pakistani community. Perhaps the most significant matter was acknowledging to an extent that intergenerational tension between young 'Pakistanis' and parents/elders exists.

The police (and other institutions) have an important role to play in the community but so do the communities and individuals themselves. Working with communities, particularly the young people, has become a priority and also with older generations as well so they are in position to understand the work that the police do and the pressures of policing in the 21st century. For too long the police have been seen as the 'other' so that it has become difficult even to have dialogue in a constructive way. Others also have an equally important role such as the elders in the community who have the daily contact with their community members. They can act as the 'go-between' and should be the important link between the community and institutions. This has to be developed and forged in order to engage with the population; the responsibility remains on both the communities and institutions.

Chapter 5

The Selection of School

'Choice for whom? The LEA or the Parents but, hey, don't I have a say?'

This section explores how Pakistani parents and children select secondary schools. The Education Reform Act (1988) transformed the British educational system. It would allow parents increased choice over the selection of their child's school (Bradley and Taylor, 2002). For the community in question the parents and the biraderi have an enormous influence. As in all communities there are many reasons why some schools are selected, while others are considered to be a 'bad' or a 'not so good' school. Much of the literature points to the examination results of schools but this research highlights the influencing cultural reasons as to why a particular school is considered to be appropriate or not. The Pakistanis, like all parents, select schools for different reasons. What was striking was that two out of six young people had 'no say' in the selection of their secondary school.

The contradiction between the parents' right to select a school for the child encouraged by the Education Acts and the child's right is clear. The issue is about who decides; the parent or the child? Over half of young people said they had a 'say in choosing the school' they attend (fifty-nine per cent). Forty-two per cent of young people assumed they had 'no say' in choosing the school that they presently attend. This was for a number of reasons. Slight gender differences were found; boys were more likely than girls to say that they had some say in choosing the school they attend (fifty-nine per cent v. fifty-eight per cent respectively). There were interesting reasons behind this.

The pupils who attend the two independent schools in Bradford, School E and School F, were most likely to have a say in choosing the school they go to now, but this only provides limited explanations to the overall picture of how selection is made. While others who attend certain schools, for example School N (Islamic school) and School H (state school), were less likely to have any say in the selection of their upper school. The results show that only twenty-three per cent of young people who attend School H and twenty-four per cent of young people who attend School N said they had a say in choosing their school. For most of these children it was the parents who decided which school was best, as opposed to the child or in some cases the LEA.

The Pakistanis, like all parents, welcomed increased choice in the selection of their child's primary and secondary school. To have the 'right' to send their child to almost any school should have pleased the parents but not all parents are happy. Many Pakistanis in Bradford feel that, although there is discussion about 'choice' being available, they still do not believe that they have 'real choice', and this is a general concern for all parents who do not get a school of their first choice. It is not a race issue. Although 'choice' is considered as something good, it can often mean something different for the parties involved, the LEA and the parents as in this case; but often overlooked in this process is the child, who will have to eventually attend the school. Where would he/she like to attend and why? Indeed does anybody ask him/her?

Parents want their children to attend a particular school because they believe their child will do better there academically. We hear of stories where parents are less truthful or even 'lie' about where they live so they fall within the catchment area of a good school. Bradford tends to do less well in the national averages and a place at a good school is keenly sought among parents, which can lead to problems. In culturally diverse communities like in Bradford, schooling opens up a whole range of issues. Some have highlighted that there are racially segregated schools and the effect that this can have on social integration of people and communities. The need to have 'integrated' schools where children from all cultures and faiths attend is hoped will overcome further segregated communities. The real issue for parents is that some schools are seen as being 'White' schools while others are seen as being 'Asian' schools, and as a result all sorts of labels are imposed on the schools.

Integration is much more than just visible or physical integration. It is about 'hearts and minds'. Children need to learn about the many cultures and faiths in a positive way. This is not just something that can happen at school but children can learn through their everyday contacts with people. The school has a role to play but so do the parents and the communities they are a part of. Some parents will almost turn a blind eye to the religious ethos of the school as long as the child can get a place in what they consider a 'good school'.

Some young people in this sample believed the system of 'catchment' works against Pakistani or Asian children in Bradford. There are some parents (irrespective of ethnic background) who believe they have little chance of attending a high achieving school, for example School K or School M, which many Pakistani parents consider as a gor-ra school (White school) and where outh-tha pan-na chang-ga (they study well at that school). Parents argue that the school league tables suggest that the examination results for the GCSE and 'A' levels are higher where the school has a majority of White children than those schools which have a majority of Asian/ Pakistani pupils. Of course not all White schools do better than those considered to have a large majority of Asian children. The important point is how such schools are seen by parents. The data suggests that Pakistani parents do not wish to send their child to a school that has a majority of 'Pakistani' children. There are many Pakistani (and White) parents who argue the system of catchment area disadvantages their young people where they are more likely to attend a 'low achieving' school, for example School I or School H. Having to go to an allocated school was another reason for resentment towards the Local Education Authority,

'I go to School I...it was the closest to us, so I got the school...I would have gone to School M' (boy, age 16)

The vast majority are allocated a school in their local catchment area, which the young people label to be a 'low achieving' school' and where 'a lot of Asians go'; and considered to be an apna school such as School I or School H. However, this was made much more difficult because most parents had little formal qualifications (and the fact that they could not hire a personal tutor either), but some found other means of getting extra tuition. Most young people realize that schools could be better. The young people had a good idea of what a 'good' school is; one that achieves good GCSE and 'A' level passes and some schools were seen better than others,

'It is a good school. I wanted to go there (School K)' (boy, age 17)

How information was gathered about schools was interesting. The young people looked at previous examination results of the school and the stories they heard from friends who were at that school, for example about bullying and truancy. This also applied to the more educated parents or those who could access information, but parents who had little knowledge of the schooling system, or who had problems associated with language, relied on older family and biraderi members for information about schools. Parents and young people are aware that some schools do 'badly' compared to both the local and the national average. This was for all sorts of reasons ranging from examination results, problems of bullying, high levels of truancy and ill-discipline. For most Pakistani parents it was important that the school had discipline and low levels of truancy.

The 'sink' schools labelled as 'low achieving schools' had an effect on the morale and confidence of some young people who clearly wanted to do well at school. The effect that attending a 'sink' school can have on career aspirations was clear for some,

'...I was thinking about my future, what future...no-one passes in the school (School K)' (boy, age 17)

This is a concern for all parents and not just Pakistanis. There are many White parents who are unsuccessful in finding a good school for their child just as the 'Asians'. The most common complaint reported centred around the system of catchment and how school places are allocated could be explained better to parents. Most young people in the sample attend schools that contain a large majority of Pakistanis. In most cases the allocated school was often third on their list of preferences, while for others it was not even on the selection list. This was seen as being unfair. According to some children, schools used different sorts of criteria: for example some schools did not accept Muslim children because it is a Christian school.

In these cases parents feel resentment towards Bradford LEA and how it allocates schools, but this should not be seen as a Pakistani issue but one that parents from most backgrounds feel strongly about. This has led to unsatisfied parents exercising their right to appeal against the decision of the LEA. Parents were also aware of reasons why their child might not get a place at a preferred school. For example the family may be recent arrivals in the area and there are simply no places left. They did not automatically appeal against the decision of the LEA. At one level this is similar to the White/English experience; the desire for their children to attend high achieving schools, but beneath the surface this reveals issues of race and gender and the preference for certain values over those of others. On the one hand many Pakistani parents consider mixed schooling as a threat to their traditional values and that it can have a corrupting influence, but on the other hand many parents believe that a gora ('White' school) can provide their children with a good education.

Labelling was used in many different contexts, particularly when referring to a certain school. For the parents it differentiated between a 'good' and a 'bad' school. Once a label has been attached it became difficult to remove. These were not just casual labels which changed over time. The next generation of parents simply re-enforced those labels which means that for example School I is labelled as,

'Well a couple of girls got caught hanging about with boys so my father said that he won't send me there (School I) so I got School H' (boy, age 14)

In the above example School H was chosen by the father, not because of its examination results, but because there was an assumption that his son would not have an opportunity to mix with the opposite sex. The following boy suggests that some children will not reach their full potential because of the school and the effect this will have on their future aspirations and his particular emphasis on 'apna' (Pakistani)

'(School I) I heard not many apna pass' (boy, age 16)

In this context the school, with its below average results, is pointed out as not being as good as some others. Parental strategies that help children to succeed at school need to be culturally specific. Those responsible for this task need to be aware of the issues affecting the different communities and develop strategies around those issues in a sensitive way. Parents also need to work in partnership with schools to achieve this. The home-school liaison teams play a crucial role in this process. Parents are encouraged to come and visit their child's school, talk to teachers, not only on specific days such as the Parents Evening sessions. Communities and schools appear sometimes to be detached from each other rather than being part of one another. Widening participation strategies that are jointly developed with parents and communities are likely to have the most effect of encouraging young people to stay on at school and also to apply to university.

Single-sex schools

An increasing number of Pakistani parents were prepared to send their daughter to a single-sex school (or a Muslim school) where there was the opportunity. Some parental differences were found; fathers were slightly more likely than mothers to insist the daughter should attend either a single-sex school or a Muslim school. This may not be the only reason why Pakistani parents call for state funding of Muslim schools. Central to the parents' main worry is that boys and girls will mix and this could lead to base-thi (dishonour) among the biraderi. Separating boys and girls at school is seen as essential to prevent this from happening.

The case for single-sex schools is almost used in a different context to how some White/English parents may view single-sex schools, where they are seen as something good that will help their son or daughter to achieve better examinations results. Single-sex schooling did not necessarily mean that the boys and girls did not mix but many parents still, nevertheless, make an assumption that they do,

'I'm at the girls' school but you can see girls go over to the boys' section talk to them; the boys are always chatting up the girls and the girls like that' (girl, age 17)

Most young people saw the benefits of mixed schooling; her father could only see the dangers that lay ahead, for example in case she started mixing with, or forming relationships with, boys,

'They think you'll mess about with boys and get a bad reputation' (girl, age 16)

The girl explains, the school can be seen by some parents as a place where one can "get a bad reputation" by mixing with boys. A "bad reputation", a stigma placed on the young person, especially a girl, is particularly difficult to remove. There is also the reality; the young know that once they leave school and get a job, they would mix with the opposite sex (and also people from different ethnic backgrounds). The more the parents dislike mixed schooling the more the young people seem to rebel against the idea. Most young people are against the idea of separate schooling. Another girl explains that it is the relatives rather than her parents who appear to have a greater say in the selection of her secondary school. These young people did not understand the need for separate schooling or at least their parents' argument for separate schools,

'My relatives want separate schools but I don't. My cousins agree' (girl, age 17)

This demonstrates the old way of thinking and the new. Others said that if they had a choice then they would prefer to attend a mixed school, for example School I. For parents the dangers are always there; allowing their daughter to mix in the 'wrong' company has its consequences, but for these young people mixing and wanting to be with friends is seen as being natural, and without moral overtones of bad behaviour. Cultural stereotypes continue to play a significant role. This is an ancient contradiction which is also exemplified in Western societies where it was also assumed that girls would remain innocent and naive until married and boys would naturally 'sow their wild oats'. Where parents see the advantages of sending their daughters to an all-girls' school the young people saw the importance of mixed schooling and one, revealing a modern attitude, said,

> 'I think we all should go to mixed schools so we can learn about each other's cultures and races so we can understand each other better' (girl, age 17)

Choice meant different things for the young people. Good examination results of a particular school was only one consideration when young people aired their preference. For example, one girl said she would have preferred to attend School I (this school was considered by most of the sample to be a poor performing school) since her friends enjoy more freedom at that school,

> '...I have a good laugh with my mates S and R especially at lunchtime when we go smoking behind the bins' (girl, age 17)

For this girl the purpose of schooling is not to pass exams but to enjoy meeting her friends and having a good laugh. For the young people who are not unhappy or dissatisfied with attending school they actually enjoy going but for different reasons. What is different from other findings is that most remain in school rather than play truant. They find ways of enjoying school despite attending classes,

> '...no-one is interested in passing exams; most are just having a laugh' (girl, age 17)

The motivation to attend school was mixed. The young people were at school for all sorts of reasons. Most wanted to be in school while others simply saw 'no point in it all'. This is reflected, to some extent, in the truancy rates and non-participation in education but parents and their community had an important say in the matter. Others pointed out the lack of interest "in passing exams" which for some is a reflection on the school as opposed to dissatisfaction with schooling generally.

Muslim schools

Dissatisfaction over educational policy has centred on providing adequately for Muslim children and there have been many calls for state funding for Muslim schools (Parker-Jenkins, 1995), which, it is argued, will raise academic standards. The 'Pakistani/Muslims' are by no means a homogeneous group; the issue would be how to accommodate the needs of all these children in the setting. The debate over under-achievement has led to a call by some Pakistanis for Muslim schools. The major argument is that Muslim schools would help to raise academic attainment of Muslims and also cater for the needs of the Muslim child. Taking into account that over the last twenty years the state-maintained education system has been subject to enormous changes, much of it has been to allow parents greater choice.

The Education Act 1993 would allow parents and other organizations to apply to the Secretary of State for their own grant maintained schools. Despite this some argue that until recently the Government has been unsympathetic to the needs of Muslim groups for the right to state funding equivalent to that available to Church of England and Catholic schools (Mason, 2000). What this research shows is that not all Pakistani/Muslim parents (and young people) are in favour of Muslim schools. The earlier Swann report (1985) concluded that voluntary aided schools would be socially and racially divisive but Muslims argue that other religious minorities such as the Jews receive state funding and this should be extended to Muslims. The views of Muslim parents were explored by Modood et al (1997) who found that Pakistani and Bangladeshi parents were more likely to have a preference for single-sex schooling for their daughters and also a preference for their own religious schools, but there is also some evidence that parents would like Muslim schools for their sons also (Dooley, 1991; Islamia, 1994).

An increasing number of Muslim children attend Church of England schools. Some Muslim parents see this as a justification to argue that the national curriculum is geared towards White/English pupils and does not take into account other cultures and religions. Some Pakistanis/Muslims argue that the national curriculum should reflect an Islamic orientation that would encourage cultural identity (Anwar, 1982; Hulmes, 1989), for example the history syllabus could reflect Muslim contributions to science. It is argued that Muslim schools will provide both the national curriculum and an Islamic ethos. Others have highlighted the concerns of parents arising out of Muslim pupils participating in dance, music and art lessons (Parker Jenkins, 1995). The reasons behind the attitudes of parents who favour Muslim schools are clear at least on the surface: the transmission of Asian and Black history in state schools.

The importance of preserving cultural identity for Muslims is where parents attempt to keep their children away from perceived Western materialism and permissiveness (Sarwar, 1983; Raza, 1993). The major fear for Muslim parents is that their British-born children will move away from their faith, culture and influence. The more the sense of traditional identity is threatened, the more vehement are the defensive mechanisms. There is no indication in this research that this is happening, in fact quite the opposite is true, most young people are adhering to the guidelines of their religion.

LEAs have made progress to accommodate the needs of Muslim parents and children. Schools have also allowed Muslim children time off from school to celebrate Eid and the provision of Halal meat in school catering facilities. Some schools have limited physical education during the month of Ramzan (Carroll and Hollinshead, 1993). Another change included parental right to withdraw their children from religious assemblies, which was enshrined in the Education Act (1944) and upheld in the Education Act (1993). Pakistanis/Muslims welcomed this move but some White/English parents saw this as a failure of the school to provide a religious ethos, albeit Christian.

The development of Jewish, East European, Indian, Pakistani and Bangladeshi supplementary schools has been the desire to retain cultural identity and has been a major motive, which in most cases is very strongly linked with the retention of a mother tongue and religious identity. Tomlinson (1984) argued that Asian parents in Britain face problems of retaining a linguistic identity which will allow all generations within a family to communicate with each other whilst at the same time ensuring that the children can operate in the language of the majority society.

Perhaps the most controversial issue to face the LEAs is school dress; Muslims are expected to maintain a high level of decency (McDermott and Ashan, 1980; Sarwar, 1994). Muslim parents insist that their daughters cover themselves by wearing shalwar and kameez and, in some cases, the hejab (Karim, 1976; Mabud, 1992). Some of the earlier concerns of Muslim parents were overcome, for example, Bradford schools would allow Muslim girls to wear trousers instead of the conventional school uniform (see Iqbal, 1975). Other schools in Bradford have excused Muslim girls from participating in mixed swimming lessons.

Parental choice can mean different things. Whilst 'choice' is part of the educational mantra of the Government, as if it were wholly a good thing, choice can also be a sign of discrimination like the phenomenon of 'White flight'. This is demonstrated by several public examples: at a Dewsbury school there was a row where White parents refused to send their children to a school with a high intake of 'Asian' children. White parents argued that the school would not be able to support the culture of the child (Gill et al, 1992; Blair, 1994). The parents in Cleveland did not wish to send their children to a school where nursery rhymes were sung in an Asian language (Gaine, 1995). The introduction of the alternative was seen as a threat to the traditional school structure. There are many others, examples of 'White flight' and the suspicions felt towards forms of Islam, or other beliefs held by minority ethnic groups themselves. One outcome is that schools are labelled as either 'White', 'Asian' or 'mixed'; schools are distinguished along the lines of race or ethnicity.

There is evidence that ethnic and racial segregation has increased through parental choice. It appears that 'choice' means offering White parents a means of avoiding schools with a high intake of ethnic minority children (Tomlinson, 1997). On the one level this is considered by some to be 'racist' yet a closer examination shows that all parents want to have a choice to select their preferred school. Muslim parents argue for Muslim schools in order to promote an Islamic ethos; should this be considered as racist? Controversy arises only when White/English parents refuse to send their child to a 'Pakistani' or 'Asian' school, but we rarely, if ever, hear of Asian parents refusing to send their child to a 'Pakistani/Asian school' or appeals on such grounds.

The parents', or the child's personal preference for a specific school is often quite different. Parents of all backgrounds would like to select a school for their child and the child in turn to accept the decision but this rarely happens. Two girls who attend the Islamic school (School N) were against the idea of attending that school but their parents had insisted. The important issue for girls was choice and being allowed the same rights as their brothers. They were often overlooked by parents. Girls that attend School N were the least likely to 'have a say in choosing the school they go to now'. This was a source of grievance for many girls who said they would have preferred to attend a school of their choice rather than go to a school of their parents' choice,

> 'I didn't have much say in it, most of my friends went to School H or School I. I wanted to go there but my dad wanted me to go to a Muslim girls' school' (girl, age 15)

At the same time her views were being ignored. It is like the child who is pushed into attending a school of somebody else's choosing and starts off with a negative attitude towards schooling. These young people do not wish to be at school for a quite different reason,

> 'I don't really enjoy it here…I told my dad I don't want to go there, he started shouting and going on about izzat and that' (girl, age 15)

Often it was the father (in other cases it was the mother) that insisted that the daughter must attend a Muslim school, again a sign of personal will against that of parents. This was a source of continual argument with their parents. They argued that many of their friends, cousins and brothers are allowed to attend a mixed state school and parents should apply the same rules to them. Attending certain schools also meant that other forms of control were imposed, however minor. The girls who attend School N mentioned that their parents, their fathers in particular, insisted that they must wear the traditional pur-kah (long black dress) at school. The girls were strongly opposed to this and it was a continual source of argument within the family home. The sense of helplessness on the part of the girls is clear. Not only were they told to attend a specific school but also they were told what to wear.

Few individuals like being told what to do, especially young people, and the consequences of this authoritarianism are clear: resentment and hostility towards parents. The lack of understanding on the part of parents is one that extended not just to the selection of school but to issues that may be considered as minor things such as the freedom to wear a different colour hejab,

> 'I have to wear a hejab and that and colours like brown, grey and black!…it's because I have to and I hate that' (girl, age 15)

Another girl reiterated a similar point: she would prefer to have the approval of her parents rather than to sneak behind her parents' backs and get changed outside. The avoidance of this is unrealistic and the lack of understanding and communication on the part of parents is clear from the young people's points of view. Having to wear a particular style of clothing had clear effects. Girls believe, as a result of being told what to wear, i.e. traditional pur-kah (long black dress), that they are regularly teased on their way to school which makes them 'very unhappy' and they 'regularly cried' at home and felt that their parents did not sympathize with their situation. The pur-kah, or the dabata (headscarf), forms part of the school uniform where some girls may like to modify or simply wear shalwar and kameez instead. This reveals a different kind of awareness when compared to most other young people who make little comment on their school uniform.

Summary

Some of the sample attended Muslim schools (or single-sex schools) while others made in-depth references to this issue. The complex reasons why certain secondary schools are preferred by Pakistani/Muslim parents were explored, particularly the cultural reasons. Muslim schools have been fostered as an idea in the Islamic community as if they were a sign of religious choice, or a backlash against the segregationist implications of 'White flight'. The actual circumstances are far more complex and ambiguous. As the research reveals the fostering of single-sex schools is not only a religious or a gender issue but also one that suggests a desire of control. The problem is that 'White flight' is often viewed as being racist; the reality is that all parents want to exercise 'choice'. The common reason for preference for a certain 'good' or a high-achieving school is better examination results and these are often oversubscribed schools. This research is different as it points to other influencing cultural reasons as to why a particular secondary school is considered to be appropriate. Attending a mixed school has other advantages: it allows them to enjoy freedom.

Chapter 6

The Experience of School

Truancy

Most schools have a percentage of children that play truant and this sample was no exception. Some schools had 'more of a problem' while others seemingly had 'very few truants' on their books. The school tables make this clear which are carefully read and interpreted by schools and parents alike. Parents often make judgements about a particular school based on the truancy figures as to its 'desirability', read closely with the examination results. All parents worry about truancy and the fear that their child might be influenced by his/her peers to play truant. Truancy is a discreet act that can be hidden by those involved. It is not only a physical separation from the school building, which is easier to measure and is reflected in the truancy rates. It can also be a psychological detachment from lessons, such as staring out of the window or not concentrating on one's work. There are differences among the various communities; for example in this Pakistani community the cultural influences that once stopped most Pakistani children from playing truant appear to have lost their influence as more and more Pakistani children appear to be playing truant. There are strict sanctions imposed on the individual and his/her family. Tackling the root causes of truancy requires all these parties to work in partnership.

The important questions are the causes of truancy and how to tackle it. Children play truant for different reasons, ranging from those who are bullied to those who appear uninterested in school. By listening to young people generally we can really understand their experience of school, what they think and, for those disinterested pupils, the purpose of schooling. There are other issues of importance; for example forcing pupils to attend school when clearly they do not wish to partake in the school life for all sorts of reasons, or in cases of disruptive pupils. All of this can have an enormous effect on the learning of motivated pupils (and of course on the class teacher). This can also create difficulties for the child who is considered to be 'disruptive'. Disruption can mean different things, from the 'class comedian' to the one who is a 'class bully'. As teachers know (and the children themselves know) it only takes one child to disrupt the whole class.

Most parents, particularly within the Pakistani community, frown upon truancy. The importance of schooling and qualifications for Pakistani parents is seen as innay rozi ditthi (they have given us a living). The purpose of schooling for most parents is clear: to pass examinations and move onto university, as is the case for boys. Parents believe that if their child attends school then he/she should be in school and argue that assa parye say pay-jaya (we sent them to school, to study and not to play truant).

They would argue that their young people who truant innay pora goriaa apna mulh honay chi-nah (they should in Pakistan),

> 'Unlike Pakistan where only the rich kids go to university and not the poor kids' (boy, age 14)

The parents of these young people value schooling as something that will help them in their future. Those young people who said they play truant openly admitted this. Several young people admitted that they truant regularly from school,

> '…we skive off from school a couple of times a week' (girl, age 16)

Similarly,

> '…a lot of my mates especially the boys don't go to lessons' (girl, age 17)

In such a community this finding is the more significant. Young people were aware of the need to be discreet in public where things may be done in secrecy. This is a naive assumption on the part of parents, that they can actually control the attitudes of young people. Nearly a third of young people said they had played truant from school/college (33 per cent). The remainder said they had not played truant (67 per cent) and the 'confession' rate is surprisingly high. Of those young people who said they had played truant, 17 per cent said they played truant 'rarely' and 11 per cent 'sometimes', but four per cent said they played truant 'regularly'. Those aged 18 were least likely to play truant from school (27 per cent), whereas those aged 17 were considerably more likely to play 'truant' from school or college (39 per cent) than from any other age. The question is why?

One common explanation for truancy may be due to the socio-economic factors but the differences in numbers who truant were not considerable. Young people from manual backgrounds were more likely to truant from school or college than those from professional backgrounds (32 per cent v 21 per cent). Young people whose fathers are pensioners were most likely to truant (72 per cent). Truancy is a common phenomenon that affects all sections of the community. One young person admitted playing truant from school,

> '…of course I have!…me and R go to town and that to mess about which is really good fun!' (girl, age 17)

and also reported a dislike of certain lessons,

> '…loads of times especially during Urdu and Games (ibid)

Some lessons were easier to 'skive off' than others because a class register was not always conducted. In other cases friends of truants would make an excuse like 'so and so is going to be late because he/she has to see the headmaster'. This would initially distract the attention of the class teacher; most teachers never checked to confirm the excuse. Some teachers were seen as 'easy to get on with' or 'cool' and the young people generally got on well with those teachers. Other teachers were seen as being 'strict' and were generally avoided in the corridor and in the playground. The 'strict' teachers were those who had set codes of behaviour in the classroom or those who ensured that the homework was done on time.

Just over half of young people said they 'always' enjoy going to school or college (58 per cent); 41 one per cent of young people said they enjoy going to school 'sometimes'; the remaining one per cent said they 'never' enjoy going to school. There were all kinds of reasons why young people enjoyed going to school. This included the opportunity to meet and talk to friends; it is a social centre (Cullingford, 1999) a place for some to enjoy themselves out of sight of parents and relatives and free from parental restrictions. Gender differences were also found. Girls were more likely than boys to 'always' enjoy going to school. Beneath the surface this reveals the far greater complexity of the Pakistani community. On the one hand girls were more likely than boys to say they enjoyed going to school, even though they are more likely to leave school or college early. The school is seen not as a means to advancement to gain qualifications but to enjoy oneself. For the parents a 'bad' school with problems of truancy and ill-discipline is a pointer for other misdemeanours at school. In such schools the objective for the parents is to get their child a good education and to get him/her through schooling without being tarnished as a 'truant'. But as all parents know 'laying the rules' can sometimes make the young person more determined.

The young people were more likely to play truant from college than school. Some schools appear to have more of a truanting problem than others, for example School D (state). School E and School F (independent) do not appear to have a problem; at least it was not reported. One reason for this may be that a further education college has a more 'grown-up' attitude where it is the choice of the student to attend classes rather than being reprimanded for 'skiving' by the teacher and reported to parents when at school. This inevitably acts as a punishment. The parents have labelled these schools as a mar-rar (bad school) and this provides some justification for the attitudes of parents towards certain schools. The disadvantages of truanting were also highlighted by those who were committed to getting a good education. For example, as one girl who had stayed on at school and, clearly encouraged by her family, continued to do well at her studies, explained,

'what's the point? I'll be leaving school with hopefully 10 GCSEs and 'A' levels, so what's the point not going to school. I'll lose in the long run' (girl, age 17)

Another made reference to the purpose of truancy and revealed the underlying motivation for truanting. She was aware what lay ahead; leaving school at 16 irrespective of her examination results, working in her parents' shop and the inevitable marriage. The lack of choice to make her decisions and the feeling of helplessness are clear,

58   *The New British*

'I know I'll be leaving and working in the shop, so the way I see it I might as well enjoy myself whilst I got the chance' (girl, age 16)

Some similarities were found; boys and girls were equally likely to play "truant' from school (34 per cent v 32 per cent), but girls were more likely to play truant 'regularly' (six per cent v two per cent), as if there were a gender backlash that reinforces the reaction to parental control. This is significant, since other literature shows that boys are assumed to be much more likely to play truant than girls. School is the one place they can hide and live out their own wishes. This is ironic because they both condone their parents' control, implicitly. There is a contradiction of acceptance and hidden rejection. Again, through experience, she is aware that her husband will 'keep an eye on you' even after marriage,

'parents want to marry their kids off especially the girls so they don't get the opportunity to mess about' (girl, age 16)

She is likely to be under more restrictions from her husband,

'They know once you're married your husband will keep an eye on you' (girl, age 16)

These habits have been long established and the influences can still be seen. For many Pakistani parents truancy reveals 'immoral' behaviour on the part of their young. For the parents the responsibility is shifted to the school to ensure that children are kept at home and if they play truant then parents must be informed. The young people are aware of the consequences if caught truanting. Common activities for truants included socializing with friends of the opposite sex, going to the cinema, eating out or 'hanging out'. In many ways the experiences of young people of Pakistani origin, outside of the family home, are not dissimilar to the experiences of young White people. They enjoy doing the same things. The fear of being caught or being seen by family or a relative was a constant worry for many girls but not to the same extent for male truants. Those involved in truanting were aware of the objection of parents and elders if they are caught truanting and the consequences, but at the same time they know these experiences are normal. The major concern among girls was that whilst playing truant they might be caught by biraderi members and not because of fear of being caught by teachers:

'we always go out of Bradford; it's safer just in case your family or relatives see you' (girl, age 16)

This reveals the influence the biraderi can have on the individual. The fear of getting caught and the effect this can have on their parents within the biraderi is clear, and so are the consequences for the truants. Despite the consequences, boys and girls still do it, suggesting that personal will prevails over the authority of parents and the biraderi. The fear of shame upon the name of the family was a deterrent for some, while most other truants took their chance. Where the consequences are clear for the parents, i.e. loss of izzat in front of the biraderi, for those involved in truanting it appears to be acceptable and almost excusable,

'They're (parents and elders) just worried about the base-thi (shame)' (girl, age 16)

Where the behaviour of the daughter can bring considerable base-thi (shame upon the good name of the family), she is labelled with a bad reputation. This does not apply to the son's behaviour. For example, if a girl is of marriageable age, prospective suitors will, in most cases, decline to make a marriage proposal on the grounds of he pooria nah meer-inni (goes out with boys) or lugg-arr aye (one who has a bad reputation). If the biraderi have labelled a specific family as a base-thi family (behaving dishonourably), the family are aware that the label will 'stick'. The young people were fully aware of the sanctions the family can impose. As one girl explained the consequences that lay ahead in the event of being caught,

'...she'll get killed and sent straight to Pakistan and get married. Parents look for any excuse to send their daughters to Pakistan, it's so unfair. It hurts but you can do nothing' (girl, age 16)

It also reveals the necessity to 'hide'; to keep as secret as possible their alternative behaviour. A number of young people who played truant in this sample were not disaffected with school (most actually enjoyed going to school) but wanted to gain greater freedom.

Bullying

The definitions of what constitutes bullying are numerous. What pupils report is not necessarily the same as the number of everyday incidents that they would put down as 'teasing' or being 'picked on', or even everyday arguments. To some extent this is an experience that is 'hidden', and a result of a clash between cultures, not only between different people, but also with internal dilemmas in the same people. The fear of being bullied and keeping safe is an important consideration for young people when they select schools (Lucey and Reay, 1998); this can be different for parents. What was clear is that bullying was common in all schools and many young people were affected by it,

'There's fights sometimes after school and inside' (boy, age 15)

Often overlooked is that bullying can take place both inside and outside of the school premises. The young people in this sample were twice as more likely to be bullied at school than outside school (seven per cent v four per cent). A number of young people have been, or are bullied (ten per cent) either at school or outside of the school premises. Another six per cent said they have been bullied 'rarely'; three per cent, 'sometimes' and three per cent were bullied 'regularly'. Bullying affected both genders; boys were more likely to be bullied than girls (12 per cent v nine per cent).

The number of young people who were open about their experience of bullying was revealing.

The effects of being bullied can have an enormous impact on the young person. Some avoid school altogether and start playing truant or make all kinds of excuses to avoid school. Most can see the school as a problem rather than the solution, especially if a bully is reported to the school and little, if anything is done. This can often make the problem worse for the child concerned. Another problem is that bullying is often hidden from family. In most cases the family only learns about the plight of their son/daughter in tragic circumstances such as when they commit suicide or harm themselves in some other way.

At some schools bullying was more common than others. The results showed that young people who attend School E and School F were most likely to be bullied (50 per cent and 34 per cent). Those who attend School G (inner city, mixed, state school) were most likely to be bullied (23 per cent). It was clear that some teachers (and schools) are taking the problem of bullying seriously.

> 'But the good thing is that the teachers sort it out…they'll punish them like detentions and that or if you keep getting into fights they'll write to your parents' (boy, age 15)

There was some evidence of racial bullying,

> 'Well they call you names like you know stuff "Paki" things like "dirty Paki". I hate that when they say that' (girl, age 17)

Although attempting to ignore the racist comments, the hurt felt by some young people hits home,

> 'I've been racially harassed by White kids, called names like "Paki" or "brown sugar". I don't take much notice of them, even though it hurts' (girl, age 16)

Being physically or verbally bullied amounted to the same thing. The reasons for being bullied are various and include racist name-calling and dress sense. For example, the two girls who attend School N mentioned they are 'regularly' teased on their way to school, especially at the local bus station by White/English children and believe that it is due to the clothes they wear; the pur-kah. Both girls mentioned that if they had the choice then they would dress in Western style clothing in order to fit in better, instead of looking 'different' and in effect they want to adapt,

> 'Especially when I bus it here from Leeds Road, especially at the Interchange a lot of the White lads are going to school like School L, School E. You get teased and that…some of the White lads pull off our hejabs; others just pick on you call you names' (girl, age 15)

Trying to fit in with others was important to these young people and reflects the general consensus among the young not to appear somehow different or look out of place. Dress was one thing that they could change. These young people did not see themselves as being any different from their White counterparts. Most did not report incidences of bullying to teachers or parents and felt they would not understand their situation or it could make matters worse. Being labelled as a 'grass' or a 'snitch' was something to be avoided since this would only make matters worse. Having older male siblings or relatives in the same school helped matters because they could offer protection against bullies.

Summary

There are many reasons for playing truant from school but these are rarely understood, especially those that are particular to minority or majority ethnic communities. Some play truant because they are bullied, while others dislike school or having to participate in certain lessons. What is clear is that many young people have played truant even if it was just once. For the community in question cultural attitudes remain a strong deterrent against those who play truant. Bullying affected many young people in the sample, which is not untypical of other research on this issue. The reasons for being bullied vary enormously. Being bullied because of skin colour was only one reason and being bullied for many for wearing the 'wrong clothes' to having the wrong kind of accent was much more significant. All of these are markers of distinction and young people are well aware of other people's differences (or weaknesses) that they are able to exploit. Most children remain quiet about being picked on at school and they often suffer in silence. However, when this issue does arise there is a need for teachers (and parents) to understand the victim and tackle the problem. All the evidence suggests that the number of those being bullied may be underestimated in research. Most young people who suffer from being bullied do not have an adult person that they can talk to or help in matters.

Chapter 7

Too Many Aspirations?

Staying on or leaving?

Most parents have an important say in their child's schooling, especially whether he/she should stay on at school or leave, but in some communities parents can almost dictate the path the child will take. Most young people had high aspirations and the desire to succeed at school. In order to do this they acknowledged the importance of continuing their post-16 education. 'Career' had different meanings and outcomes for boys and girls. It also highlights the important role parents play in the lives of their young people, not just in their schooling but also in all other areas such as employment.

There is an enormous amount of research on non-participation of young people in education and employment, most often linked to their socio-economic position. This has been the focus of much debate, but there are many reasons why individuals leave school. Some do not like schooling itself and others simply want to take time out and enjoy being young without the pressure of studying for exams and perhaps return later. For others parental and community pressure play an enormous part in the non-participation to the point that they have too many aspirations to achieve.

The majority of young people had decided whether they would be intending to stay on at school/college or leave when they participated in this research. A high proportion of young people of Pakistani origin intended to continue their post-16 education (46 per cent). A further twelve per cent of young people said they will be 'staying-on', 19 per cent said they 'will be leaving' school/college and only a small minority of young people, four per cent, had not decided on either option. Gender differences were found; boys were more likely than girls to stay on at school or college or will stay on (52 per cent, 16 per cent v 41 per cent, nine per cent). This raised broader issues that affected girls generally. The majority were intending to 'study for a degree' (66 per cent) after leaving school or college. Some findings were common with other research where young people from professional backgrounds were considerably more likely to 'stay on' at school than young people from manual backgrounds (69 per cent v 48 per cent), but the picture is much more complex. It is argued that like in any community norms and traditions play a crucial role, more than socio-economic background, in whether the child succeeds at school and whether he/she stays on at school.

Some occupations are clearly regarded as having a higher status than others, such as medicine, and parents typically want their children to enter these professions. Those young people who were intending to do science degrees realized that they would need extra help in terms of private tuition in order to get the GCSE and 'A' level grades. This was not a reflection on the school they attend but the general difficulty in getting very good 'A' level grades. Some parents were in a financial position to help pay for extra tuition while others would like to help but it was simply out of their financial means. Parents were clearly behind pushing their children to succeed. The willingness to do well is clear for most young people,

'I want to do science because I want to do dentistry after my A's' (boy, age 15)

At the same time some of those aspirations, such as studying for a prized dentistry course, will go unrealized. Many had too many aspirations or different expectations. In some cases boys were 'forced' by parents and the biraderi pressure to ensure that they continue their post-16 education. Like most parents a place at university was prized, something that all the biraderi will hear about not just in England but also in Pakistan. The situation was different for most girls. Post-16 schooling was often viewed as a one-year 'stop gap'. Despite the awareness of their expectations girls were willing to carry on studying for a one-year course even though they were aware they would be still expected to leave school or college. For some girls there was little choice to make decisions about their immediate future. Pakistani parents continue to make the most important decisions on behalf of their young people, such as continuing one's schooling and future expectations. At the same time these decisions were accepted as being inevitable; something that could not be abandoned or even delayed. The following example was typical of many girls and their predicament,

'I know I'll end up getting married when I'm 18 or whatever' (girl, age 18)

Attitudes of some parents were a source of grievance. Most of the tension lay in the fact that brothers of girls were encouraged to stay on at school/college and go to university. Realizing that culture plays a dominant role the young people involved often used Islam to argue their case. Islam insists that every individual must have the right to seek knowledge and education where the acquisition of knowledge is an obligatory one for every Muslim, both boys and girls (Doi, 1989). Girls were, however, aware that these occupations can remain a dream,

'I'd love to go to university...I'd love to be a teacher or a nurse' (girl, age 17)

Despite the parental expectations the desire among girls to do well at school was clear,

'I know mostly girls they want to do well at school' (girl, age 17).

Statistics show that girls perform better in examinations than boys. There are all sorts of reasons why they do. Schools play a vital role but so do parents. The girls who wanted to do well in this sample were either supported by their parents or were committed to do well without their parents' support. Those who received little encouragement were demonstrating to parents and the biraderi they could do just as well as, if not better than, their male counterparts. As the girls point out they do better academically than boys because they spend more time indoors after school and they use this time studying while the boys spend much of the evening playing outside with friends. Many boys were aware of their sisters' situation. The feeling of helplessness is clear for many young people. The young people realize from a very early age what will happen to them in the future. All seems planned and thought out by parents,

'They want my sister to stay at school until 18 and then they are not that bothered. After that she'll be marrying my cousin from Pakistan' (boy, age 15)

The end result, in some cases, can be seen from the alternative forms of employment caused by low educational attainment. For example home working, i.e. sewing clothes for friends and relatives, especially in the case of young Pakistani girls. The crucial factor is to understand the different communities and how they support their young people during their schooling. Of course there are some situations that parents with all the good will in the world find difficult.

Importance of qualifications

Most young people agreed that 'having qualifications is important' A total of ninety-five per cent of young people believe that 'having qualifications is important' as opposed to six per cent who said 'having qualifications was not important'. According to young people their parents also believe that having qualifications is important. Ninety-six per cent of young people believe their respective parents consider 'having qualifications as important'. For most young people staying-on at school, the link between having qualifications and increasing their employment opportunities in terms of getting a 'good job' is clear. They view qualifications as opening up new opportunities for employment,

'there's not many jobs around so 'A' levels are really important' (boy, age 14)

Also the connection between a son who does well at school and izzat for his family,

'...they want their kids to do well because it's all about izzat and that' (boy, age 18)

For those families who want their children to do well the importance of obtaining qualifications and the affect this has on the izzat of the family is enormous. Parents know they can have a 'high status image' around the success of their son. If the son is from a high caste obtaining qualifications re-enforces their status in their biraderi. But if an individual is of a lower caste obtaining qualifications increased the family status. Succeeding at school/college through examination passes meant considerable izzat for the family. Another notes the connection between 'respect' and 'izzat',

'…they feel proud of you, it means a lot of respect and izzat from relatives' (boy, age 16)

Respect is personal: izzat is a more general accolade for the whole family. By contrast, failure at school can mean there is a 'price to pay', which can be reflected in the loss of izzat of the family where relatives and biraderi members refer to the parents and their children with inna-nay mo-ray ghoria ne mena-nay (their sons and daughters do not study). Failure has dire consequences, and this loss of izzat can have a lasting effect on the individual, who feels he may have let his family down,

'…that even puts pressure on parents and parents in return want their kids to do well because it's all about izzat and that it's a vicious cycle which you can't get out' (boy, age 18)

The traditional expectations were pointed out on many occasions,

'They want you to get married, arranged have kids sons firstly, get a good job and earn lots of money and build houses in Pakistan' (boy, age 19)

A number of girls explained that there would be little point in obtaining academic qualifications since they would be leaving school at 16, 17 or 18. This could account for the six per cent of those young people who do not think that having qualifications is 'important'. Although the definition of what is meant by 'care' was left to the young people, most young people said their parents 'care' about their sons and daughters 'doing well at school or college' (74 per cent v 26 per cent) in terms of their education. This is not surprising as most parents in any community would say the same, but there is, however, one common distinction to be found: boys were much more likely than girls to say their parents 'care about them doing' well at school or college (91 per cent v 58 per cent). Achieving qualifications becomes of little use since even after marriage she will remain within the home. The clash between aspirations and reality is clear,

'not that important…'cause I know I'll end up getting married…so what's the point?' (girl, age 17)

At the same time she realizes the plans her parents have made. The desire to succeed at school is clear but at the same time she realizes that some of her aspirations will remain unfulfilled. For many girls (and in a small number of cases boys) this reveals a lack of motivation to achieve examination passes at school or college,

'Definitely not! If I had the choice I'd do my 'A' levels. I think I'll pass my GCSEs and go to university…I'll be getting married before that I'll be staying home' (girl, age 16)

Intended destination

Most young people (66 per cent) were intending to 'study for a degree' after leaving school or college. Six per cent were intending to leave school to find 'work'; eight per cent to start 'work for family'; ten per cent would 'stay at home'; eight per cent were getting 'married'; three per cent were intending to 'go abroad'; one per cent mentioned 'self-employment' and one per cent had definite 'no plans'. Gender differences were found: boys were considerably more likely than girls to say they 'intend to study for a degree' (85 per cent v 49 per cent). By contrast, girls were more likely than boys to find 'work' (eight per cent v four per cent); 'work for family' (ten per cent v six per cent); 'go abroad' (four per cent v one per cent); 'stay at home' (18 per cent v zero per cent) and enter 'marriage' (thirteen per cent v two per cent). Schooling can be seen by some parents as a threat to the traditions.

There were some socio-economic differences; for example, those who attend School E and School F (independent schools) intended to 'study for a degree' after leaving school. By contrast, young people from manual or manual related occupations were more likely to leave school at age 16. Like the majority, the life chances differ enormously according to socio-economic status and school. These young people had been clearly supported by their parents and wanted to do well,

> 'They (parents and relatives) want me to carry on and be successful, they encourage me a lot' (boy, age 19)

Another made a similar comment about the differences in intended destination of boys, the support offered by family and the need to do well,

> 'They're all for it. I get a lot of support from family. They want me to do well like my brother' (boy, age 18)

This was different from the experience of some other girls. A number of girls challenged their parents over their decision to take them out of school or college. In reality most girls would continue their schooling but only for up to two years after post-16 before leaving and 'staying at home', 'working for family' or 'getting married'. The majority of young people were studying towards 'A' levels (forty-nine per cent) and GCSEs (36 per cent). The remaining were studying towards other 'A' level and GCSE equivalent courses, i.e. GNVQs, B/TEC and NVQs. Gender differences were found: girls were more likely to be studying GCSE and 'A' level equivalent courses, i.e. NVQs (five per cent v three per cent) and GNVQs and (ten per cent v two per cent) than boys, but boys and girls were equally likely to be studying B/TEC (five per cent v five per cent). The lack of real choice over individual futures is clear, where other people decide what is best for her but at the same time realizing there is little some girls can do,

> 'It was meant to be a year's stopgap. My father and mother said I could go to college for a year. No, I'll definitely be leaving' (girl, age 19)

And what lies ahead is equally clear,

> 'I'll be going to Pakistan, stay there for a while and get married to my cousin N' (ibid)

There is the suggestion that she had accepted the decision taken by parents to leave school after the completion of the present course, go abroad to Pakistan and get married. She states that she will 'get married to my cousin N'; it is as if her future plans have been decided for her. This also highlights the continuing hold of traditional attitudes,

> 'well you should ask my father, he says that a woman's place is in the home looking after the husband and kids' (boy, age 14)

Such attitudes were areas of tension, as was the reaction where rules are considered as being unfair. This girl has clearly thought about what she wanted to do rather than what was expected of her,

> 'I don't want to stay at home when I'm married, I want to work' (girl, age 17)

The influence of the biraderi over parents was also clear,

> 'It's not just my father that says I must leave but also my relatives, their daughters have left school. They don't think it's izzat or good for a girl to stay on at school' (girl, age 16)

There are also differences within the many 'Pakistani' communities. In some families and biraderis it is expected that both the son and daughter will attend university, while in other families boys are encouraged to find work as soon as possible after leaving school. Any job is considered to be better than being unemployed. This would usually mean manual employment, i.e. restaurant worker or taxi driving due to their lack of qualifications, or entering the family business if the opportunity exists. From a Western perspective for example driving taxis or working in a restaurant is seen as low occupations but among some Pakistanis they view it as an achievement.

The employment patterns appear to be similar to their fathers'. Leaving school with few qualifications has a knock-on effect on the type of job these young people would get. Some of the opportunities to 'better' themselves through getting a decent education are lost. The ones who leave school early do not appear to return to education at some later stage. This has a psychological effect on those concerned and the inevitable regret, that 'I wish I had stayed on at school and worked hard' or 'only if had the support'. There is the other reality where, despite having qualifications it does not guarantee a job, never mind a prized one. The following boy explained the dilemma faced by some young people,

'My father wants me to work...my father bases this on that a lot of people who have degrees haven't got a job or are working in manual jobs, so what's the point?' (boy, age 14)

Success meant different things. For some it meant working towards, and gaining, qualifications, while for others it meant starting work as early as possible after leaving school. Qualifications were not the only way to succeed financially as many older Pakistanis have demonstrated by having set up their own businesses. It is a cultural heritage to become self-employed. Very few early Pakistanis had any literacy skills in English or in Urdu for that matter but went on to become entrepreneurs.

Some boys wanted to emulate their fathers' success in setting up a business or buying houses to rent-out. They used their fathers and uncles as role models to motivate themselves in that anything was achievable through hard work and determination. They wanted to spend the early years after leaving school working to get some money together and gather 'ideas' about which business would be likely to succeed. The 'family' would provide most of the financial backing and readily available 'helpers' who would work voluntarily to get the business off the ground. 'Success' was often visible such as having a house (or indeed several houses) or a new car and it was both measurable and identifiable. For some of these young people and their parents starting work early was a way of achieving those goals. As the above quote shows having qualifications did not necessarily mean financial security or even a graduate job. This is put down to non-participation of young people, but as we look closer those who leave school (mainly boys) early often look for other opportunities.

Many Pakistani parents did not attend Parents' Evenings and this was a concern for teachers and schools. Differences were found in terms of which parent attended; twenty-two per cent of young people said their father attended the Parents' Evening meetings and was more likely to attend than the mother. Only 11 per cent of young people said their mother attended. A breakdown showed that five per cent of fathers attend their sons/daughters' Parents' Evening meetings, 'sometimes', 12 per cent 'regularly' and four per cent said their fathers 'always' attend; and in terms of mothers, the data showed that four per cent of mothers attended the meetings 'sometimes', six per cent of mothers attended 'regularly' and three per cent 'always' attended.

The low attendance at Parents' Evening meetings by Pakistani parents should not lead to an automatic assumption that these parents are less interested in their children's schooling. They are typical of some other communities. This can be due to a number of reasons: the inability of mothers and fathers to communicate in English, which can act as a barrier between some Pakistani parents and the school and teachers. Fathers were more likely to attend Parents' Evening meetings than mothers. One explanation for this may be due to better communication skills of Pakistani fathers than mothers, having gained these skills through their longer stay and interaction with the wider British society, for example contact through employment, DWP, schools and hospitals. But this does not mean that all parents with language difficulties do not attend Parents' Evening meetings as there are many mothers and fathers who go along with their children and where the children act as interpreters.

Many schools encourage parents to come and visit and chat to the headteacher and the teachers. There are wider cultural factors that may explain the reasons why parents are nearly twice as likely to attend their sons' PE meetings than their daughters'. Many schools in Bradford have made enormous progress to accommodate and reflect the needs of those parents who speak little, if any, English especially during home–school contact. The home–school liaison teams largely reflect the ethnic origin of the pupils. They provide the crucial link between the school and parents but also are key workers in the community and often act as interpreters to parents. For some the school is rarely seen as an extension of the home but a place where children simply go during the day. The purpose of school is rarely explained to young people or indeed to parents generally.

We need to look at ways of encouraging parents to visit their child's school. Some parents have never visited their child's school, while others only visit when problems have arisen such as absenteeism. The issue is that most parents do not know much about the school, never mind what actually goes on within it. One way of encouraging parents who lack the confidence in contacting the school themselves or those who have language problems is for the home–school liaison teams to contact parents themselves. Another is to arrange workshops in school for parents to come along to and find out about issues relating to schooling prior to the school term. Workshops can used to build relationships with parents and the community and where parents feel they are taking an active involvement in their child's education.

Summary

Much of the existing research shows that the socio-economic background is a major factor in whether the child continues post-compulsory schooling or leaves. The results presented here show that, as in most communities, there can be cultural factors that can be equally or more important than one's socio-economic background.

There is an important relationship (rather than a partnership) between the school, the parents and the child. In order for the child to succeed this relationship has to be fostered and understood. Whilst the child is at school the teachers and the support staff have an important role to play and equally, at home, the parents (and the communities they are part of) have to support their young people. There is also a duty for teachers and others to be aware of (and understand) their students, and where they are coming from. These should not be seen as different worlds but rather as interlinked with each other.

Chapter 8

The New British

Young people and identity

The *Bradford Commission report* (1996) is typical of most reports. It acknowledged there is a problem with using terms such as 'Asians' or 'White' when defining a specific population. There is no term that would accurately describe children and grandchildren who were born and educated in Britain. Despite this admission most continue to use the same terms as those which are used to describe their parents, suggesting that a racial rather than a cultural version of stereotyping was being used. Whilst the Bradford Commission was sensible in acknowledging that there are problems associated with describing young 'Pakistani' children who are born and educated in Britain in terms of their identity, it did little to correct them. For example, terms such as Pakistani, Kashmiri and Muslim were in some instances inaccurately used, often interchangeably. This highlights the very same 'sins' of labelling that the report criticized.

The term 'Pakistani-born English' should be a more appropriate term (or indeed for any other community. Despite the reservations the Bradford Commission accepted that it would still be appropriate to use the term 'Asian' to describe young Pakistani people. This highlights the flaws in the report, that at the outset young 'Asians' could 'feel' that even though they were born in Britain they are still regarded as 'Asians', and not British. The concept of 'grouping' communities is far more complex and elaborate. Despite these problems the Bradford Commission attempted to simplify the question of identity without attempting to tackle the problem, in particular by describing young Pakistanis who are born in England as 'Asians', without regard to the validity. There is an institutional (and academic) difficulty in describing children of immigrants who are born and raised in England (or in the UK).

Individuals and communities choose to describe themselves in different ways. For some this becomes a problem when their preferred description does not fit in with predefined categories. These categories are used to make the job of describing easier but it leads to communities being treated as homogeneous without taking into account differences or indeed similarities between groups. Often overlooked is the way in which the 'White' communities are homogenized for the purposes of research which takes little account of the differences within the 'White' category, for example those who are Welsh, Scottish or Irish. Some members of the minority communities, especially the young people born in England believe that identity is imposed on them and they have little say in the matter. There are a number of examples which highlight the change in labelling; we have had a number of titles used to describe people whose parents' country of origin is Asia. This includes terms such as ethnic minority, minority ethnic, Black minority ethnic, Asian Pakistani, Pakistani-British, British-Asian, Asian-British or worse, abbreviated as BME. This problem will continue with the expansion of the European Union and also the arrival of asylum seekers will add to the difficulty. These terms incorporate many different communities and cultures.

We also need to be aware how individuals, as part of larger communities, describe themselves. In the community in question, there are other descriptors that are applicable, such as Kashmiri, Pakistani or, for those who come from the urban parts of Pakistan, Islambadian, Lahoreri and Karachian. All of these groups think of themselves as being different from one another. It is like those from Yorkshire and Lancashire who consider themselves as having almost a different culture, never mind the so-called divide between the North and South. There may come a time when geographical position, rather than cultural distinction, will be the mark of nationality but even this statement can be open to question. The term 'British' shows to some extent an uncomfortable middle point in referencing.

There is a constant shifting of identities, particularly among the young, which takes into account the changing circumstances (Inglehart, 1990). However, individuals tend to be seen in terms of groups, for example caste and class, or of region and nation (Cullingford and Din, 2006) which does not adequately take into account either the differences or indeed similarities. There are many forms of political and religious communities (Seton-Watson, 1997). Identities can be expressed through many manifestations. Sport provides an appropriate illustration of particular ethnic and national loyalties, for example through football matches between England and Germany or in the Six Nations rugby match between England and France. This indifference or even hatred is common throughout (Wright, 2002). Sport is an integral part of the nationality debate, for example Tebbit's cricket test.

Identity is also geographically dependent. Research into second-generation Indo-Caribbean young people's ethnic identity found that they have multiple influences on their identities. For example in terms of clothes and movies girls are interested in things 'Indian', whereas boys tended to distance themselves from an Indian identity (Warikoo, 2005). Bjorgo's (2005) study into neo-Nazi gangs found that youth groups often switched between political identities and gang identities depending on the situation. There are noticeable differences between genders; Dion and Dion's (2004) study of immigrants in Canada found that women tended to endorse their ethnic identity, for example around issues of maintaining cultural practices, more than men.

Young British-born 'Pakistanis' are part of many different social, religious and cultural identities. Identity is fluid and changes over time. This is rarely acknowledged, for example in the National Census and in research that categorizes individuals and groups into 'old' commonly known demarcations such as 'Asians' or 'Pakistanis'. These individuals are part of multiple identities. This can be a result of external and internal tensions. This can also create difficulties within minority ethnic communities, for example within migrant communities. Young people are often part of a 'cultural supermarket' (Hall, 1992) where individuals choose from various identities which are visible in society. That positions individuals in their social context (Deaux et al, 1995).

'Ethnicity' is used for many purposes, particularly research which should enable institutions and organizations to provide an ethnically sensitive service. It is an outcome rather than a process of how individuals (and communities) identify themselves and which identity they see themselves as being part of. One aspect of inequality is how the external processes of definition are imposed on minority groups (for example groupings such Pakistani, Asian or BME) by the majority which allows for individuals to distinguish themselves from 'others'; this leads to exclusion (Nazroo and Karlsen, 2003). On another level this could apply to 'minority within minority' communities, for example members of one religious sect view themselves as being higher than the next one maintaining hierarchies. Identities can be both inclusive and exclusive of others, discriminating at will. There is 'internal definition' where individuals and groups define their own identity (Jenkins, 1996). At the same time individuals are constrained from choosing an identity by external factors (Smaje, 1996). Ethnic identity can also be a political tool to further a group's cause; it acts as a social movement (Solomos, 1998).

Although ethnicity is just one part of identity this has been the focus of much research over the years (see Ahmad, 1996; Smaje, 1996); class and gender can be more important in some situations than ethnicity (Nazroo and Karlsen, 2003). Identity should be considered as being neither secure nor coherent (Hall, 1992). For Hall the process of globalization plays an important role where local identities are forged even more strongly for others cultural traditionalism particularly for minority ethnic groups. This can also lead to a new 'hybrid' (Hall, 1992a) identity where identities are adapted or merged with others. For example in the case of migrant communities, while maintaining aspects of their own culture and traditions, they become part of new cultures. An appropriate example is Jacobson's (1997) study of young British-Pakistanis in London. She found that religious identity was more important to the young people – identities such as 'Pakistani'. However, 'Muslim' identities can be a resistance to racism (Nazroo and Karlsen, 2003).

Most 'English' do not see themselves as being part of an ethnic community and therefore will not develop an identity based on this (Baumann, 1996). This can equally apply to the Europeans (Banks, 1996) where identity is rather more fluid than static. National identities are connected with local identities and based on cultural symbols and histories (Hall, 1992). The national identities are continually changing, for example in the UK the mixture of 'White' people from Scotland, Wales and Northern Ireland as they exert their identities on the English in terms of music and culture. Not forgetting the 'Asians' and the influence on English society ranging from food and curry to music and culture. However, Jenkins (1997) argues that the ability to act is dependent on power or the authority to act.

The question of identity/nationality is one of the most debated issues, especially at the present time with closer links with the rest of Europe and tragic world events such as 9/11 and 7/7. The issue of youth identity has become increasingly important

especially among young Pakistanis (Muslims). Factors such as class, sexuality and
ethnicity are important to understand how identities are changing (Rattansi, 2000).
In academic circles at least there are signs of change from describing non-White
immigrants as 'coloureds' to the study by Modood (1997) that found the majority
of young people described themselves as 'British' as opposed to 'Pakistani'.
However, most are willing to accept those very same titles for their own categorical
convenience. Racial categorization can lead to separateness (King, 2005).

Few young people describe themselves as 'Asians' and most describe themselves
to be culturally British, which was supported by references to their appearance,
forms of socializing and choice of entertainment (Modood, 1997; Stopes-Roe
and Cochrane, 1990). Ghuman (1999) found that an even higher percentage of
respondents than the Modood (1997) study (74 per cent of young people) regard
Britain as their home country and more than half believe they are 'British'. The
huge investment, for example the building of mosques, is one indication of both the
commitment by Muslims to stay in Britain and the determination to pass on to their
children their religious and cultural values (Lewis, 1994). Ramdin (1999) found
that young Asian people living in Scotland considered Scotland to be their home.
Their commitment was demonstrated by building schools and places of worship.
Self-labelling by individuals as regards their identity is important given the multi-
cultural nature of the UK (Parekh (2000a). For some this suggests that a decline in
British identity affects values or the idea of a multi-cultural citizenship (Condor et
al, 2005).

There is evidence to suggest the creation of hyphenated identities along the lines
of the US situation: for example bicultural terms such as 'Asian-British' or 'Scottish-
Asian' are used more commonly (Aspinall, 2003; see also Watson, 1977). However,
there can be resistance to assimilation of cultures and identities which leads to
instability of hyphenated identities in Britain (Rattansi, 2000). Differences are to be
found within the UK: the use of hyphenated identities is common in Scotland, for
example Pakistani-Scot (Modood et al, 1997).

Identity can be demonstrated through various means. For example, language
is an important marker of identity. Ibrahim (1998) states 'not only identities are
reflected in languages but also constructed in, through and within them'. Tomlinson
(1984) suggests that a motive behind the development of Jewish, East European,
Indian, Pakistani and Bangladeshi supplementary schools has been the desire to
retain cultural (and linguistic) identity, which in most cases is very strongly linked
with the retention of a mother tongue and religious identity. She argued that Asian
parents in Britain face problems of retaining a linguistic identity which will allow all
generations within a family to communicate with each other whilst at the same time
ensuring that the children can operate in the language of the majority society.

Asian-American teenagers often use slang as belonging to African-Americans,
while others authenticated identities as slang speakers (Reyes, 2005). Similarly,
Giampapa (2001) found that Italian-Canadian youths often negotiate their identities
through language where identity is continually shifting, i.e. Canadian, Italian-
Canadian and Italian) or through music and the preference for certain types of

popular culture (Din and Cullingford, 2004). There are also modern influences on young people such as technology which gives young people identity (Kroger, 1989). There is also 'New Technology' identities, for example mobile phones, which reflect a young person's identity both individually and collectively as a part of wider group (Aakhus and Katz, 2002).

Muslim identity

Religious identity has become particularly important to understand because it often demonstrates loyalties towards particular issues (Cullingford and Din, 2006) or even causes. It is only until recently that 'Asian' people have emphasized their Muslim identity (Scantlebury, 1995). Much of this changed in light of the *Satanic Verses* by Salman Rushdie ensued by public demonstrations and book burnings that allowed a collective (Muslim) identity (Glavanis, 1998). Other deep-rooted factors for some appear to be that a 'Muslim identity' may also act as a defence against living in an alien culture (Sarwar, 1980; Mohammad, 1999) and also resistance of ideological pressures placed on individuals (Hylton, 1997). This collective representation is an example of mutual benefit to be had by individuals (Ringmer, 1998). This collective consciousness is part of an ethnic identity (Browning, 2001).

Numerically at least a 'Muslim identity' will become a major force in all spheres of social, economic and political life in the UK and also across the globe. It can also be a source of strength (Moyende, 1997) especially when one is aware of the difference between his/her identity and that of others (Dorsett, 1998). A 'Muslim identity' in all its manifestations has largely been the result of the declaration of war on terrorism in 2001 by British and American governments; there has been a revival of Muslim identity which since has been associated with citizenship and nationality (Archer, 2003). Muslim identity is by no means a homogeneous category and many contradictions are located within this which in the West cross-cuts diverse socio-political identities (Salih, 2004). There are differences among the generations; for example some young women choose an ethnic identity while others focus more on religion than ethnicity (Walseth, 2006). Islam, like other religions, is exclusive (Ansari, 2004); however White people do not appear to be labelled as having a 'religious' identity like Muslims. However, Youniss et al (1999) found that religion plays a dominant part in the lives of some American youths.

Young Muslim girls can also reflect their identity through dress (Dwyer, 1999). Dress is also a mark that the individual is representing more than just him/herself (Varshney, 2002). In light of 9/11 'Muslim dress' particularly the *hejab* has become an important signifier in the lives of young Muslim women not only in the UK and US but across the world. They can be fused into the broader categorization of a 'Muslim' identity. These can be described as the 'new' British Muslim identities (Alibhai-Brown, 1994). As addition periodic visits to Pakistan can also create a self-awareness about one's inherited cultural values (O'Neill and Cullingford, 2005). There may come a time when geographical position rather than cultural distinction will be the mark of nationality, but even this statement can be open to question. The term 'British' shows to some extent an uncomfortable middle point in referencing.

Despite all the terms used the majority of young people in this sample make clear that they consider themselves as 'British' as opposed to 'Pakistani'; 87 per cent said they describe their identity as 'British', 11 per cent said they describe their identity as being 'Pakistani' and two per cent as being 'English'. All these young people (boys and girls) were considerably more likely to describe their identity as 'British' (87 per cent and 87 per cent respectively) than 'Pakistani'. Some differences based on age were found. As the age of the young person increases, the more likely they are to describe their identity as being 'British'. Those aged 14 and 15 years were less likely to say they are 'British' (73 per cent and 83 per cent), whereas those aged 18 were most likely to say they are 'British' (91 per cent). Young people aged 15 and above were more likely to describe their identity as 'British'.

The important question is what does 'British' or 'Britishness' mean to these young people. It is a term that encompasses people who are part of different and distinct communities, e.g. the English, Welsh, Scottish and the Irish. In any multi-cultural society this term can apply equally to those born in the country with inheritances from various countries in Europe and from Hong Kong, Africa, the West Indies or East Asia or maintaining an identity deliberately, such as the Jewish community. Individuals and communities in different parts of the island have their own definitions and their own criteria of what 'Britishness' means. At worst we think of differences that are particularly brought about through 'ethnicity' or 'ethnic' data highlighting how 'ethnic' people are different from the 'White' rather than many of the similarities that exist between them. These young people believe they are British in terms of where they regard 'home' suggesting that traditional attitudes of many elders are questioned and being eroded by many young people who consider Britain to be their home as opposed to Pakistan. A change of attitudes is clear between the generations. The consensus was clear,

'Well we're British and Britain is our home' (boy, age 18)

They spoke about their preferences and choices in terms of where they wish to live, but what was once considered as the 'host culture' has become part of their heritage culture. England is regarded as 'home' and where they want to be, as the following girl points out,

'I consider England and Britain to be my home, so it's everything' (girl, age 17)

It is natural that most young people born in Britain would consider it as their home. Their attachment to Britain is strong and increases as the level of adjustment grows. These young people have clear and well thought out criteria by which they measure what it means to be 'British'. This includes the preference for the use of English language, food, music, literature and dress, to name but few, 'like I dress in English clothes, I wear trousers, skirts, I listen to English music and watch English films' (girl, age 17)

Similarly another pointed out,

'They (young people) definitely think they are British, gora (British), that everything about them is gora, even food they want to eat chips, pizzas instead of chapattis and also they behave in a gora way and wear British clothes' (girl, age 16)

These criteria are much broader than the one introduced by Norman Tebbit, the Conservative Member of Parliament, which attempted to measure the loyalty of 'non-English' people residing in the United Kingdom by using the 'cricket test'. The test was to ask 'non-English' people a simple question: which cricket team would they support if England were playing Pakistan? (Mason, 2000). On this issue 63 per cent of the young people said that they would support Pakistan in the Cricket World Cup if they were playing England and the other twenty-seven per cent of young people said they would support England. But what does this mean? Supporting Pakistan in cricket does not necessarily mean that these young people believe they are 'Pakistani'. People have a preference for football teams from another city or even support a team from another country. Many people from Yorkshire support Manchester United, a team from Lancashire; does this mean they are not 'real' Yorkshire people? What was striking was the sense of loyalty and commitment the young people and parents have towards Britain.

The majority of young people consider their parents to be 'Pakistani' in terms of their identity. This did not mean that they considered their parents to be any less loyal to Britain than the young people. Some obvious differences were found in terms of socio-economic background. The data showed that professional fathers were considerably more likely to describe their identity as British than fathers from manual backgrounds (76 per cent v 28 per cent), whereas manual fathers were more likely to describe their identity as Pakistani (seventy-three per cent v twenty-five per cent). At one level many older Pakistanis would describe their identity as being 'Pakistani' purely because of their sentimental attachment to Pakistan, Yet their parents are as 'British' as young people. It also suggests a superficial divide between 'us', i.e. Pakistanis, and 'them', i.e. British, and also the hidden belief that one culture is superior to another, or that it is an advantage to make use of both.

Parents and Identity

Young people were also clear and explicit about the identity of their parents. Seventy per cent of young people believe their father would describe his identity as 'Pakistani', 29 per cent as 'British' and the remaining one per cent as 'English'. By contrast, 85 per cent of young people said their mother would describe her identity as 'Pakistani', 14 per cent as being 'British' and none of the mothers would describe their identity as being 'English'. The following was typical of what most young people said about their parents,

> 'My father would say British, he's been here most of his life…as for my mother she would say more Pakistani than Britain' (girl, age 17)

Another points out,

> 'I think that these bud-day (older Pakistanis) are as British as young people (boy, age 18)

This demonstrates how earlier social trends, like fathers coming to Britain and the mothers staying at home, have been perpetuated. We do not, however, see the same distinction between the newest generations. For many young people the length of time in Britain, the ability to speak English on the part of their fathers, and increased contact with the wider British society and institutions were important factors. It is interesting to note why most young people indicated why most parents would say their identity is 'Pakistani'. For example, in terms of attitude and their way of thinking, the preference for arranged marriages, as opposed to the Western concept of the 'freedom to choose', which of these would young people clearly like to see their parents adopt,

> 'They'd say they're Pakistani, definitely Pakistanis…it's all the things they do and say, like Pakistan is our home, they build houses, send money to Pakistan. They also want us to have arranged marriage[s] which the Pakistanis born in Britain don't want' (boy, age 19)

The young people have a clear definition of who is considered as a 'Pakistani' when 'they build houses', 'send money' and have an 'arranged marriage' in a distant land. Many of their natural thoughts go back to their parental origins, a process that is being eliminated over here by the younger generation. Many older Pakistanis regularly visit Pakistan. This might perpetuate the ties but the majority of British Pakistanis stay in Pakistan for a relatively short period of time, usually three or six months and then return to Britain,

> 'My father goes to Pakistan for holidays but he considers Britain to be our home' (boy, age 19)

The closeness of their parents with relatives in Pakistan continues with regular visits to Pakistan for a holiday, wedding or funeral. These visits might well be cultural reminders but there is a deeper shift of emphasis. In addition to this visiting, contact is also maintained through regular telephone calls, letters and sending gifts. Sending remittances remains popular among many Pakistanis especially those from the rural parts of Pakistan. Remittances are sent to support family and relatives back in Mirpur through building family homes, acquiring businesses and property. There is a natural attachment to those relatives still left behind so it would be naive to assume that older Pakistanis could simply detach themselves from Pakistan. Another example, which illustrates the commitment of Pakistanis to Britain, can be seen through marriage. The majority of young people apply for an entry visa to join their spouse in Britain and do not wish to remain in Pakistan after marriage. There are a number of reasons. The economic benefits are obvious but close family ties are now more clearly made with those in Britain.

The majority of Pakistani parents believe that 'en-na gora rose-ze dhiti-thi' (these White people gave us a living). Also many Pakistanis view every 'positive action' as building closer ties with Britain, especially the granting of entry visas for their son or the daughter-in-law. There is general acceptance by the older generation that Britain is their home.

'...like my father can speak English, so they're intelligent they know they'll never move to Pakistan and have accepted it' (girl, age 17)

On the issue of 'home' there appears to be an acceptance by parents that it is unlikely they will return and settle in Pakistan,

'...but none of us have been there (Pakistan)...my father knows that we'll never live there (Pakistan)' (boy, age 18)

Significantly whilst there might ostensibly be a choice about leaving Britain this is not a realistic one. These young people believe their parents' close contact with relatives in Pakistan is likely to decrease over the years. The young people interviewed believed they had little connection with family members in Pakistan, while many older parents view this attitude as worrying. The sense of belonging in Britain is clear,

'Well my father would say British because he's lived here a lot longer in Britain. He's worked here, he can speak English and all that. My mum can't, she always says Pakistan is better than Britain. My father says we're here to stay, this is our home not Pakistan' (girl, age 16)

The young people reveal increasing levels of adjustment and attachment to Britain, for example through language skills; employment and the length of stay.

Summary

These young people are clearly British and Britain is their natural home but there are problems of acceptance, not so much with the old British but their own community. This suggests that maintaining old barriers has created difficulties for the new British. Some older Pakistanis still consider the British environment as alien but at the same time they maintain loyalty to UK in all its forms. However, this causes problems for the young who have adapted to their circumstances and who feel at home in society.

For many parents there is continual sentimental attachment to Pakistan with relatives left behind. The old values remain, for example the preference for arranged marriages; at one level these remain unchanged. This suggests that some members of the Pakistani community are unwilling and unsure how to adapt to these changes of attitude. This does not mean that older Pakistanis are not committed to Britain. On the contrary vilayat (Britain) remains 'the land of dreams' for most Pakistanis.

Chapter 9

Boyzone and Bhangra: The Place of Popular and Pakistani Culture[1]

There are numerous studies that have examined young people and their preference for music, films, books and magazines they enjoy reading. The problem with existing research is that it has examined young people as a homogeneous group; we know little of the preferences of young people of Pakistani origin and their likes and dislikes. For example do they enjoy listening to English or Asian music and what kind of films do they enjoy watching? This chapter explores the tastes of young Muslims, both as they present themselves under the influence of their parents and biraderi, and their attitudes to majority tastes. The effects of different pressures on the young people, and the way they manage them, are explored.

These young people have a definite preference for, and enjoy listening to, English music and watching English films. They also enjoy reading English magazines and books as opposed to Asian literature, but it is not just about certain types of popular culture; we need to know why they prefer one type of culture over what is considered to be their or their parents' 'native culture'. The evidence presented here also reveals something about their preference for the English language over their 'home' language and also about their identity. On another level, and a theme that runs throughout, are the attitudes of their parents and their community towards what they consider to be the White/English popular culture, which for most is quite different from their young people. This also created disagreement in the house about what is acceptable in terms of which music is listened to or the types of magazines read. This is similar to the attitudes of most parents of any ethnic background about the exposure and the influence of popular culture on their children, particularly on their daughters. For the community in question it is also about their young people losing their home culture and taking on board the Western influences.

Bhatti (1999) found that girls were interested in 'pop' literature and film stars that formed part of the teenage culture generally, but for girls it was part of a covert culture as far as their parents were concerned. Bhatti found that the parents of girls would object to them looking at pictures of film stars. In addition girls were not

---

1   This chapter has appeared as a Journal paper: Din, I. and Cullingford, C. (2004) 'Boyzone and Bhangra: The place of popular and minority cultures', *Race Ethnicity and Education*, Vol.7, No.3, pp. 307-320, September.

allowed to display posters of film stars or pop stars in their bedrooms since they are unacceptable to their parents and girls left the books in a locker at school.

There was a clear divide between what young people like to watch and what they are allowed to watch, at least when at home. The majority of girls said that they are forbidden to watch English films and listen to music, whereas only a minority of boys were likely to express this opinion. Young people mentioned that their parents enjoy watching films, especially on satellite. Popular channels include Zeetv and Primetv (which show Bollywood films). They listen to songs on popular radio stations including Sunrise Radio. Parents made attempts to control what the young people viewed whilst the young people are in their company, but it is naive to suggest that parents actually do control what young people watch. However, like all young people they watch and listen to their own tastes in English music when parents are out of sight. There is a great tension in the camouflage that the young are using, leading a double life.

Music

Social statistics show that one of the most popular pastime activities is listening to music. In a multicultural society like Britain the preference for certain types of music, and indeed films, is more diverse than ever. The lack of research on minority groups and their cultural tastes is puzzling. The results reveal the close relationship between English music and personal identity of young people of Pakistani origin. Thornton (1995) suggested that the cultural form closest to the majority of British youth is music, finding that ninety-six per cent of British youth between the ages of 16 and 19 listened to records and tapes. Government statistics such as Social Trends, which provide statistics on the UK population and include figures on popular tastes such as music, television and leisure activities, showed that listening to music on the radio, listening to records/tapes/CDs is one of the most popular home-based leisure activities among both males and female (Social Trends, 2000). In terms of music listened to, the majority of young people said they enjoy listening to English music (81 per cent), i.e. pop, dance, rock, metal or rap as opposed to listening to Asian music only (three per cent), i.e. Bhangra, Qawali. The remaining 17 per cent of them said that they enjoy listening to both English and Asian music.

Like most young people they were willing to try different varieties of music before making up their minds about what they prefer to listen to. They listened to some types of music occasionally, for example Qawali during Ramzan or on Eid, whilst other types were listened to much more informally and frequently, such as pop music. Music was also a popular topic of conversation among young people and boys and girls would talk about the latest CD to be released whilst on their way to school or during school hours. Some types of music were much more 'cool' to listen to and to admit in public, like 'rap' or 'gangsta' music, which was particularly true for the boys; and for the girls it was more 'pop' music like Boyzone. Some formed friendships based on a similar taste in music. What was surprising is that, despite their enormous interest in music not one individual said they had been to a concert to see their favourite artiste or group. Perhaps this was not out of choice but the restrictions placed on them, particularly the girls.

Despite the objections of some parents accessing music was not a problem for these young people but they did not always go to a music shop to purchase a CD; instead many would download music directly from the Internet. This perhaps reflects a more general trend, while others would exchange or borrow CDs from friends. This could be done much more discreetly than going to the city centre store to purchase a CD and is another way of using the new technologies to get round parental disapproval. Where the boys could openly display their liking for music the girls would largely keep their preferences hidden from parents but they found their way round parents.

Both boys and girls were equally likely to listen to English music (81 per cent and 82 per cent). However, some slight differences were found; girls were more likely than boys to listen to a combination of English and Asian music (nineteen per cent and fifteen per cent), whereas, of this small number, boys were more likely than girls to listen only to Asian music (five per cent v one per cent). Both boys and girls were exposed to English and Asian music at different times of the day and in different contexts. Listening to music is a favourite pastime of both young people and parents. Most young people listened to English music either on their own, in the company of friends or while out of sight of parents who would object.

Most parents enjoyed listening to Asian music on the radio or they would watch Asian music videos on satellite during the day and in the company of either relatives or friends; and, like the young, listening to music is a social activity among the older generations. This was a common activity particularly among women whose husbands may be at work. It gave them a chance to meet up over tea or lunch to talk about the family, prospective marriages and what is generally going on in the biraderi. This is a source of emotional support and a base for economic support, although one does not always necessarily lead to the other.

In most cases parents would do this while their children are at school, while other parents would watch the Asian channels in the evenings with their children, especially the younger ones. The younger children would have less of a say in terms of what to watch but just because the children sat with their parents did not necessarily mean they enjoyed listening to Asian music (or watching Asian films); it was because their parents were in charge. These young people would tell their parents but as their children get older they would naturally exercise their own preferences. In this sample some older respondents had two or three televisions in the house and this would mean more freedom in terms of what they could watch and when. At the same time this would be a reflection on the relationship between some young people and their parents where they could be sitting in different rooms watching television, or indeed sitting in the same room watching television without communicating. The lack of communication between the generations is clear.

It was interesting to note a number of gender differences: girls were more likely than boys to listen to 'pop' music (90 per cent v 78 per cent), dance (42 per cent v 33 per cent) and Bhangra (16 per cent v 15 per cent). Boys were more likely than girls to listen to rock (18 per cent v three per cent), metal (13 per cent v two per cent), Quawali (six per cent v three per cent) and rap (37 per cent v 25 per cent). This is perhaps a reflection of the more general trend based along the lines of gender. What is surprising is the number of girls who enjoy listening to rock and rap songs typically perceived to be a male thing. The young people could read and understand the lyrics of those songs in English, whereas songs in Urdu or Hindi were nearly impossible to make sense of. There was a language barrier.

More than a third of boys and a quarter of girls admitted to enjoying listening to rap music. Pakistani parents strongly disliked rap music because of its explicit lyrics about violence, drugs and gangs but not all rap music is about these issues and can be along the lines of pop/rap. It demonstrates the knowledge of parents about certain forms of music and its connotations. These parents do not live in their world, isolated from what is happening around them with all their greater knowledge and experience; they attempt to channel their young away from certain influences.

Another reason for the 17 per cent of young people who said they enjoy listening to both English and Asian music may be the result of some Asian singers who have incorporated a combination of Western type pop/dance music into traditional Asian music such as Qawali. Qawali is religious music listened to and enjoyed by generations of Pakistanis. The late Nusrat Fateh Ali Khan provides a good example; he mixed Western music into Qawali music, with considerable success that reached both traditional Qawali listeners and also the younger audience, especially through his collaboration with Peter Gabriel; but very few young people enjoyed listening to Qawali music compared to most young people who enjoy enjoying listening to 'pop' music. The liking of Qawali music does not appear to have been passed onto the younger generation as most parents would have liked. Qawali is an incorporation of religious stories told by the way of a song and music. This has religious significance, but listening to Qawali was not considered to be 'cool' or something to 'brag about' with friends. Although some enjoyed Qawali they tended to keep it hidden from their friends to avoid being teased. Music was like wearing designer clothes or the latest trendy footwear and it was something to show off about.

The importance of listening to music, not just to 'Asians' but people from all groups, has always existed but many Pakistani parents have refused to accept English pop music on the grounds that it is immoral. Listening to music has always been a favourite hobby of young people (and old) the world over. There is a common concern for parents of all ethnic backgrounds about the lyrics and content of some music and music videos which their young people are exposed to. Despite all the objections by parents, the young see it differently. A theme that is echoed on many occasions is that the vast majority had a definite preference for listening to English music as opposed to listening to Asian music. A girl admits to never having listened to Asian music and this is surprising,

'I don't listen to Asian music I never have' (girl, age 17)

At the same time she proudly admits to listening to English music,

'rock, pop and that' (ibid)

Of course there are 'rock' and 'pop' songs in Urdu and Hindi but these young people prefer to listen to those types of music in English. For these young people it is not important whether the singers/groups are White/English or Asian; the important thing is that they sing in English. There have been a number of Asian singers and groups that have broken into mainstream music charts, such as Bally Sagoo and Babylon Zoo. It is predicted that even more Asian young people will go on to become major artistes in their own right and this can be seen from watching any of the popular Asian terrestrial music channels. It suggests the shift away from traditional expectations of young people to become singers instead of doctors and engineers and this poses problems for the older generation. Music was seen as an activity to be enjoyed rather than having any physical involvement. Succeeding in school and university was seen as the ultimate goal, as we have seen in the earlier chapters.

Music is a natural entertainment for most young people of Pakistani origin and part of the everyday culture of listening compared to the number who said they enjoy reading books. In this way their tastes are similar to their White/English counterparts. Perhaps more revealing is that all three examples above enjoy a mixture of British and American bands and the amount of exposure to Western music. This is a more general trend of the liking for and enjoying of British and American culture. The preference for listening to English music was echoed by the vast majority of boys and girls, their tastes being similar to any young person,

'...like Take That, Boyzone, 3T stuff like that' (girl, age 17)

'I really enjoy listening to English music, especially Westlife, Boyzone' (girl, age 16)

Note the preferences of the above two girls who enjoy listening to boy bands. They did not mention any female singers/groups they enjoy listening to, this reflects the general attraction of young girls to boy bands They do not include any boy bands but those that are British or American as opposed to Asian (Urdu or Hindi singing) boy bands. Again the following boy, who also enjoys listening to boy bands, similarly did not mention any favourite female singers. His choice of music appears to be more original rather than manufactured pop,

'I like groups like REM, Manic Street Preachers, stuff like that' (boy, age 17)

The popularity of some Western bands is famous the world over. Some of them regularly tour South East Asia and more commonly Japan. The singers/groups of course sing in English as opposed to Japanese and despite the obvious language barrier they are very popular; but this is in contrast to the young people of Pakistani origin who do not wish to listen to most types of Asian music because they cannot understand the language.

Girls were more likely to say that parents restrict them in terms of what they can and cannot listen to but few, if any, restrictions are placed on their brothers. In this sample no boys said parents restricted them in terms of music or films watched. Girls said they argue with parents over the issue of music, which for parents has a corrupting influence on them. This does not mean that girls did not listen to English music; simply that they are forbidden to do so by their parents. In fact they do listen discreetly when their parents are out of sight. Whilst seeming to concede to their parents' wishes they continue to do the things that they enjoy,

'My dad don't like us listening to English music…they're so backward' (girl, age 15)

The objection is towards listening to 'English' music as opposed to 'Asian' or any other kinds of music. From the parents' point of view this is understandable and they want to ensure that their young people are not exposed to unsuitable music. This is similar to having 'parental advisory' stickers on the front of CDs that parents, or anyone buying the music, needs to be aware of, or parental guidance notices before the start of an 18-rated film or the watershed times used for television scheduling. These go some way to ensure that parents know about the suitability of programmes.

Some have found that parents reject Bhangra music on the grounds that it encourages mixing of the sexes and it exposes Muslims to alcohol and sexual permissiveness (Hiro, 1991; Lewis, 1994). The large Bhangra discos that appeared in the late 1980s only increased parental dilemmas. There is also a predicament for many Muslim parents of how to preserve the sense of community (Werbner, 2002). Young people see all of these things as being normal and part of their everyday life. Most parents, irrespective of religion and ethnicity, would object to some performers who may use offensive words in their lyrics, but Pakistani parents object to all music that is written in English. Morality is based on contradictions; whereas Hindi film songs can also contain offensive language, this appears to be acceptable. It is not a Muslim objection but a Pakistani cultural objection. Britain is seen by some as lacking in cultural and religious purity compared to Asia (Gifford, 1990).

Films

Like listening to music, watching films is a popular activity among young people. Hendry et al (1993) found that young people watch a considerable amount of television and videos in their homes. Data from the *General Household Survey* shows that the most popular home-based activity is watching television. The majority of young people enjoy watching English films as opposed to watching Asian films. 'English' films were movies in the English language; this included those films made in the UK and also in the United States. All others were considered to be foreign movies whether they were in Urdu, Hindi or in any of the European languages.

A total of 78 per cent of young people said that they enjoy watching only English films, one per cent said they enjoy only Indian films, two per cent said they enjoy watching only Pakistani films and 19 per cent said they enjoy watching a combination of English, Pakistani and Indian films. Slightly more boys than girls said they enjoy watching English films (81 per cent v 75 per cent); however, more girls than boys said they enjoy watching a combination of English, Indian and Pakistani films (22 per cent v 16 per cent). It is clear about the types of films they enjoy watching. More girls than boys enjoyed watching romantic (84 per cent v 37 per cent) and comedy films (79 per cent v 60 per cent). More boys than girls said they enjoy watching Westerns (29 per cent v three per cent); science fiction (48 per cent v 15 per cent) and horror (48 per cent v 23 per cent). The definite preference for watching English films was asserted by most young people in the sample but this was also the view of their friends,

'English films definitely!' (girl, age 16)

Again the dislike for the alternative was reiterated,

'Asian films go on and on and I can't understand them anyway like my mates' (girl, age 16)

Ghuman (1994) states that the majority of young Pakistani people do not watch Pakistani/Indian films or videos and those who do watch them do so in the company of their Pakistani parents. This suggests a cultural shift but also a dual attitude as they publicly submit to their Pakistani parents' taste but privately prefer their own. They quickly form the opinion that Asian films are not for them by only watching clips of these movies,

'I've seen clips of Asian films at my relatives and on Zeetv' (girl, age 17)

This is not only in reference to films but also other forms of popular culture such as music and magazines. They were not rejecting all things 'Asian' but those aspects they felt they have little in common with. Like all young people they pick and choose their likes. The fear on the part of parents is that their young, especially daughters, will copy their favourite singers and actors. Parents do not accept that watching films is inevitable and natural, as is pointed out by the following example,

'My dad's uptight about letting us watching films, he thinks that they are a bad influence' (girl, age 17)

Again the 'bad influence' of films is reiterated but this does not appear to extend to Pakistani or Bollywood films which many parents enjoy watching. Basit (1997) found that most parents seemed to have a considerable hold over the kind of programmes that their daughter could watch. In her sample the majority of female respondents were not allowed to watch television after 9pm or watch television programmes and videos that parents considered to be unsuitable for them. Basit showed the reciprocal relationship between parents and children was not everything that is portrayed as 'cultural clash'.

It can also reflect a general concern among many parents at the levels of decency on television, but for the community in question these concerns often lead to excessive control on the part of parents. The young see this as unreasonable and as part of their culture. Talking about what happened in last night's Eastenders or Coronation Street is a topic of conversation for most young people in the playground. These young people did not want to be left out or to be seen by others as being somehow different or watching anything different.

The difference between the 'public' behaviour in front of parents and the private becomes evident. Once parents are out of sight, a different behaviour and what the young do is clearly observable yet ignored by parents. It is as if parents believe that young people will continue to behave in the same way once they are out of sight. Another girl points out the determination to continue with, as well as hide, her pleasures,

> 'I can't really watch English films like I say my dad's quite bad unless he's working at the taxis my brothers get some films and that for us to see' (girl, age 15)

The role of the father in laying down the rules is clear, but what of the role of the mother? The stereotypical view of the Pakistani family is that the father is an authoritarian and respected figure. In this way the evidence presented here suggests a similar story, but others point to the domineering role of the mother and not the father. As pointed out in the above quote the girl, with the help of her brother, finds her way round restrictions imposed on them. She stays at home while her brother is sent to the video shop to rent a movie. Some parents are aware that this is happening in these situations and the wife takes over the role of her husband to keep the siblings in line.

Being told not to listen to English music or watch English films made the reaction of boys and girls more resentful; personal will won over the authority of their parents despite the strong objection if they are found out doing something 'wrong',

> 'I still do listen to English music in my bedroom and watch what I want like English films, especially when mum and dad are working in the shop' (girl, age 16)

What is striking is that many older Pakistanis believe Western culture is immoral. What this reveals is their superficial control of the actions of young people as if they can be 'told' what they can or cannot do. Young people will simply follow their own perceptions of reality, which is often quite different. The young want to be honest with their parents about what they do when they are alone or in the company of friends. Few people, especially the young, like to be told what they can and cannot do. When they accept the logic they submit, but if they cannot understand it it becomes a sign of a deeper discontent. Being forbidden to watch English films the young simply thought of how to get around restrictions and at the same time hide their tastes in the company of parents,

'But we find our way around things' (girl, age 19)

Consciousness of different cultural outlooks was also quite subtle. Even in those ethnic films that the young people were allowed to see they would perceive hidden messages such as freedom and independence, especially in reference to marriage and the 'fight for love'. For example the freedom to choose their marriage partner, love and independence from the biraderi are the main story lines in classic Indian movies such as Raja Hindustani (1996). Even their own culture, and especially the Quran, can become a strong argument against the control of their parents. This was frequently used in all areas of their lives where issues were clouded by cultural attitudes.

Most young people in this sample were exposed to Asian or Bollywood films where an increasing number of the homes have access to Sky and Cable and the many Asian channels. Most often parents watched the Asian channels during the day when children were at school and in the evening some young people are allowed to watch soaps and drama but in the company of parents or elders. For many young people this places them in an awkward position. Having the responsibility of the remote control to switch to another channel during scenes of nudity was common. Many Pakistani parents subscribe to Zeetv and Asia Net. A general observation is that in households where parents are not working watching Zeetv and/or Asia Net is a favourite pastime for the mother, father and elderly relatives. It is almost a symbol of maintaining a cultural inheritance which is refusing to acknowledge the mainstream environment, a circumstance that their children and grandchildren constantly face.

Tensions can also mean double standards, which the young people are quick to point out. It almost becomes a cliché 'that they are watching what they like then why can't we',

'You know they should come in to the school to ask how their kids are doing in school instead of sitting at home and watching Zeetv!' (boy, age 14)

Bhatti (1999) found the only leisure activities discussed by parents were watching Indian films on video. These are the opinions of Pakistani parents and represent the 'official' attitude of the biraderi. The amount of control, in terms of cultural hegemony, remains both powerful, defended and insisted upon. It is as if the children are beginning to see their inherited culture, and their parents' expectations, as somewhat alien. The attitudes of parents were seen as being contradictory. On the one hand the majority of young people are forbidden to view films and listen to music, yet at the same time they know their parents and relatives enjoy watching those that fit their own taste.

Books

Fewer than half of the young people said they enjoy reading books. Reading books was the least favoured option for these young people compared to reading magazines, listening to music or watching films. In total forty per cent of young people said they enjoy reading English books only, two per cent said they enjoy reading Urdu books only and five per cent said they enjoy reading both English and Urdu books. It was interesting to note the majority of young people do not enjoy reading any books (53 per cent), which perhaps reflects a more general, majority view.

Gender differences were found: boys were more likely than girls to say they enjoy reading English books (50 per cent v 30 per cent). More girls than boys said they do not read books (62 per cent v 44 per cent). In terms of preference, more girls than boys said they enjoy reading romantic books (23 per cent v four per cent) and comedy books (15 per cent v 12 per cent). More boys than girls said they enjoy reading horror (19 per cent v ten per cent); Westerns (three per cent v one per cent) and science fiction (32 per cent v seven per cent). Clearly, these distinctions mirror general social trends – the distinctiveness of the majority.

They have a definite preference for reading books and other literature in English. One explanation is the inability of most young people to read Urdu, a language which they must learn like any other since most Pakistanis speak Pakistani and not Urdu. These young people are more fluent and conversant in English, (like music and films) and feel more at ease with the English language and its literature. The reality was quite different and there was almost an acceptance by parents that their young people would not be able to converse in Pakistani and/or Urdu. This concern extended beyond language and this is an indication of their belonging to and being a part of British society. This makes most Pakistani parents more defensive and threatened by outside influences. Losing one's heritage language was a sign of a permanent shift towards their children's culture. There is an enormous sense of sadness that Azad Kashmiri Punjabi, Urdu or any other language has not been passed on to the next generation. That young people prefer to speak English rather than their mother tongue may be due to their limited skills in that language. To many young people their mothers' language, i.e. Pakistani, is a second language. This is natural; an inevitable shift.

Magazines

Most young people (65 per cent) said they enjoyed reading English magazines only; one per cent enjoyed reading only Asian magazines and the remaining nine per cent enjoyed reading a combination of both English and Asian magazines. Girls were more likely than boys to say they enjoy reading English magazines (72 per cent v 58 per cent). Reading magazines is clearly a popular activity for many young girls, who were more likely than boys to read different types of magazines. These were *Smash Hits* (54 per cent v 16 per cent); *More* (20 per cent v three per cent); *Sugar* (22 per cent v five per cent); *Just 17* (57 per cent v nine per cent) (these are magazines that cater for young teenage girls and include stories and advice on relationships, make-up, music, clothes and fashion). They also included *Cineblitz* (11 per cent v six per cent) and *Movie* (eight per cent v three per cent) magazines. These include new film releases from Bollywood as well the latest news on Asian film stars.

Most parents consider that any form of literature such as girls' magazines could influence their young, especially girls. It is the latent message that is being put across by the magazines that parents argue is 'immoral'. They contain advice on relationships, pregnancy, make-up, dress codes, hairstyles and advice on the opposite sex. Most parents often naively believe that if they can limit or totally reduce the exposure of such material, then young people would not want to copy their peers in terms of dress code, hairstyles, music and having relationships. This suggests the tension between ostensible control and the actual hold on the imagination of young people. Control is favoured as a symbol of social order; the imposition of will over tempestuous youth. On the one hand control is attractive but, as all parents know, control and over-authoritarianism is resisted.

Girls were particularly open about why they enjoy reading English magazines: because of the advice and problems pages, especially as regards relationships and other issues such as make-up, dress, music and films. Clearly what many parents see as being immoral, the girls saw as natural,

'...anything and everything, girls magazines on make-up, clothes, boys etc' (girl, age 17)

Similarly,

'All sorts I like reading girlie magazines like *Just Seventeen* stuff like that' (girl, age 15)

Others pointed out that if their parents (especially their father) found English magazines in the house they would strongly disapprove and confiscate them. Where rules are seen as being unfair the consequences are clear: conflict and tension between the parents and young people. Having to hide in front of parents was common among most young people but once out of sight they resumed doing what they enjoyed. Reading magazines is no different from the rest of the population, especially among the 15–24 age group (Social Trends 30, 2000). Magazines were borrowed from friends and read during school time and rarely brought home because the risk of being found out was far too great. The girls who engaged in this activity enjoyed going to school and often before the start of the school day would sit and read the magazines with friends.

Access on the Internet may create other problems: despite parental supervision and parental controls that can deny access to any of the more suitable websites it is often more difficult to keep an eye on what young people access. This has particular problems for those Pakistani parents who have limited English language skills since they cannot read the web pages to determine the suitability of the site and instead they often rely on the children. Parents are often pushed into purchasing a computer and a connection on the Internet by siblings who insist that it will help them in their studies, but problems can occur if the Internet is used for other purposes.

The widespread availability of PCs in the home and greater access to the Internet means that most young people can have unlimited access to material such as music, video releases, relationships and latest fashion trends at a touch of a button without the knowledge of parents. They either access this information at home or elsewhere. Parents are not in a position to confiscate the offending material but can only limit the amount of time their child is on the Internet or exercise close supervision, which can be difficult. The Internet allows e-mails to be sent to any location at any time, which has made communication easier and more discreet than, say, using a telephone. Exchanging messages through chatrooms is another concern and the dangers have been highlighted through a number of high-profile cases. As the Internet deepens its influence on the population, the ability of young people in general to subvert their parents' authority by using digital means is likely to increase.

Interests and hobbies

Like all the young people in this sample they had various interests and hobbies that they enjoyed taking part in. Where the boys could engage in most types of sports with their parents' consent, the girls were on occasions forbidden to take part in sports such as swimming. Swimming was a 'grey' area for some, whether girls could take part or not. There is a religious objection, where Muslim females must not show any part of the naked body in public, but single-sex classes appear to be acceptable. This was a view accepted by most parents.

The most popular choice of sports/hobbies was badminton, which 41 per cent of young people said they enjoy playing, followed by cricket, which 40 per cent said they enjoy playing. This is another version of the 'cricket test'! Gender differences were found: boys were more likely to enjoy playing traditional 'boys' sports, for example cricket (74 per cent), football (53 per cent) and snooker/pool (42 per cent), but this did not mean that girls do not enjoy playing some or all of the above-mentioned sports; quite the opposite. As an example 14 per cent of girls said they enjoy playing football, but on the whole girls were more likely to say they enjoy playing what are regarded as 'girls' sports, hockey (17 per cent) and netball (37 per cent), partly because they were not always allowed a free choice on sport.

Parents did not object to their daughters or sons participating in any sport whilst at school. This would be left to the school and teachers to decide. This also demonstrates the liking for traditional sports but few mentioned other types of hobbies like playing games on their computer. The concern over issues of appropriate sports kit appears to be resolved by taking into account the wishes of Pakistani/Muslim parents. Schools allow Muslim girls to wear tracksuits during PE and Games. Similar codes have been adapted to the school uniform that allow Pakistani girls to wear a shalwar under the skirt/trousers. This is the outcome of dialogue between schools and parents. Bradford is seen as an example for other Local Education Authorities to follow.

Despite the preference of young people who participate in sport 26 per cent of them said they are forbidden by parents to participate in sports/hobbies. School was the one place where the majority of girls (who are more likely to be forbidden than boys: 47 per cent v four per cent respectively) could participate in their favourite sport without having restrictions imposed upon them. There were several common reasons why some were forbidden to take part in sport. Sport is something that is done in the public domain. Parents were worried that girls may not be able to look after themselves if confronted with a threatening situation, i.e. like in school where the teacher will be looking after their welfare. Crime or the fear of crime was a major factor in the decision whether to allow the girl to pursue outside interests. On the other hand the boys could venture outside because they would be with friends and able to look after each other if something happened.

Many parents who forbid girls from participating in sport use the religious argument but beneath the surface cultural beliefs are evident, especially when not a single boy said he was forbidden to take part in sports. But some types of sports raise other issues,

'Yeah, I enjoy swimming but my dad don't allow it anymore he says Muslim girls should not show their naked bodies in public' (girl, age 17)

If this is a religious objection, the young people adhere to and listen to their parents' advice. This was not something that they would challenge. The question is whether the suspicion of sport, as an activity, is as important as the lack of deliberate nurturing of talents of minority ethnic groups, some of whom are already playing various sports for England. The General Household Survey showed that boys are more likely than girls to take part in sports, games and physical activities. The data shows that snooker, pool or billiards were the most popular activities for men, while for women it was keep-fit, yoga and swimming (Social Trends, 2000). Minority ethnic people are less likely to attend sporting events such as football matches. The general consensus among many Pakistanis is that racism at football grounds is a major issue, together with the likelihood of attracting violence because of their skin colour. Playing cricket and football is, on the other hand, a popular pastime of many young Pakistanis. Despite this it is interesting to note that not one young person mentioned that they attend a sporting event of any kind.

Bilingual, Multilingual or just plain English?

Language has become an important issue for debate and controversy centring on the need to promote English language classes for non-English speakers, more specifically for spouses who come from abroad. The ability to converse in English is also seen as being essential to promote integration, but what are the opinions of this minority ethnic community and which language do they prefer to use?

The situation has changed enormously since the first immigrants arrived in the UK with little knowledge of English. Most of those got by without really learning English. One reason was because they resided in enclosed communities and had little contact with the wider society. They would shop at Pakistani grocery shops, use Pakistani butchers and Pakistani travel agents. For the vast majority this was a way of surviving, not just in a different country, but in one that had a different religion, culture and norms. Like most immigrant communities the Pakistani community became defensive. This appeared to work well, but would lay the foundations for what is termed a problem of 'race relations' or integration. These minority ethnic communities became so independent or self-reliant that they rarely sought to build relationships with other communities. This would equally apply to the White majority. Few people at that time saw this as a race-relation problem but thought more along the lines of a settlement process.

The vast majority of British-born Pakistanis are not bilingual but multilingual. Their first language of preference is English. Most young people in this sample could speak Azad Kashmiri Punjabi and Urdu at varying levels of fluency. Fluency in the language should be the important factor in determining whether the individual has a real ability to speak two or more languages. Although most young people in this sample said that they could speak two or more languages, when asked to simply write their name in Urdu or give directions in Azad Kashmiri Punjabi, most were unable to do so. Even counting to thirty in Urdu or Azad Kashmiri Punjabi proved to be difficult for most. There was an assumption that they were naturally bilingual but in fact they were fluent in English only at varying levels. Other young people could also speak several dialects that they managed to pick up at home or from their friends. Most young people in this sample picked up other languages through interaction with peers. Counting the number of languages one speaks is easy but acquiring a level of competency in those languages is much more difficult to attain.

Being multilingual, albeit limited, allows these young people to communicate with other Pakistanis from different parts of Pakistan, particularly with the elders. They do not just learn about the language but about the people, the traditions and culture. It is common for Pathans to mix with Pakistanis and Gujaratis to mix with Islambadians. The young see multilingualism as a positive thing. It also allows individuals who are part of different communities to communicate with each other. This is a basis for integration and community cohesion.

Some outside the community almost assume that Pakistanis 'speak the same language', or worse still that the only languages spoken are Urdu or Punjabi (without making the distinction between the many variations of 'Punjabi'). They rarely think of them as being multilingual. The young are homogenized as speaking the 'native' language; but is this English or Urdu? For others bilingualism or multilingualism is seen as those who can speak French, Spanish or the many European languages but rarely the Asian languages. This can lead to a hierarchy of languages, where some are seen as 'better than others'. This is not the way most Pakistanis think of language. They are all equal and important depending on the context. It was interesting to learn that some young Pakistanis in this sample made the point that their White/English classmates thought that they would almost certainly pass their Urdu 'A' level without too much trouble since it was their home language or their 'mother tongue'. This was of course untrue. At the same time no one expected their White/English classmates to pass English language 'A' level since that is their home language.

Most young people in the sample preferred to speak in English when conversing with friends and when accessing popular culture. Some were more fluent than others. For example those born in England and those who were born in Pakistan (who often spoke 'broken English') and girls were more fluent in English than boys. Some spoke English like their White/English counterparts while others spoke less fluently. For most young people in the sample Urdu or Azad Kashmiri Punjabi is a foreign language. It is a language that is used with parents and older Pakistanis. It is a foreign language because it has to be learnt formally like any of the modern languages taught in school. The vast majority will learn to read and write Urdu while at mosque as opposed to being taught by their parents. A concern to some older Pakistanis was that Urdu was being used less and less and this could lead to Urdu becoming a language of the past. For the young who had learnt Urdu they used it as a spoken language as opposed to writing purposes. In the early sixties the ability to write Urdu was essential in maintaining contact with relatives in Pakistan through letter. The vast majority of people did not have an access to a telephone in Pakistan, but now the vast majority of contact is made through the telephone and fewer Pakistanis write home.

The languages used are dependent on the context. However, when in the company of British-born peers they conversed in English but when in the company of parents and elders they reverted back to their parents' native language. They make this distinction clear, but most clearly have difficulty with their native language because they simply do not have the appropriate levels of skill to speak it fluently. The older generation realize this and accommodate the lower level of fluency but point out the need for their young to learn or improve on their existing level. Most are able to move from one language to another as situations change, from English to Punjabi. On this point, Stopes-Roe and Cochrane (1990) found that young people spoke in their native language only when they engage in a conversation with other family members and preferred to speak in English to each other as opposed to Urdu. 'Asian' parents mentioned that some young people are unable to speak their own 'home' language.

Some believe that Pakistani women who join their husbands in the UK are prevented from attending language classes or indeed from doing anything that involves leaving the house, but the picture is far more complex and some are actively encouraged. Others are allowed independence without the need to rely on family or relatives for interpreting purposes. Some are prevented from attending language classes. Some individuals simply do not want to learn English. This is similar to some White/English people who may not want to learn another language.

Fluency in English is seen as something that will help them in life without the need to rely on interpreters, as most of their parents did. The young people highlight the difficulties faced by their parents and elders when they arrived in the UK having little or no knowledge of English, and the barriers they faced when accessing schooling, employment and the Health Service. The ability to speak English is seen as a status symbol. It is something to be proud of and is respected both by the biraderi here in the UK and also in Pakistan. An even higher accolade is passed on to individuals who arrived from Pakistan and learnt English here in the UK. The biraderi quickly learns of the success, that so and so has learnt to speak

English. Most Pakistani parents accept that learning English is essential to bringing up children and communicating with them in their preferred language. Others see this as interference where 'outsiders' impose on a minority ethnic community the requirement to speak English, but these young people see all languages as being equally important. They are exposed to all kinds of languages and dialects from which to choose their preferences.

The national language of Pakistan is Urdu and tends to be spoken by those who have received some elementary schooling (Matriculation or 'Matric' as it is commonly known), but not all Pakistanis can read and speak Urdu unless the individual is a native speaker. There are many variations and many more dialects that are used both in rural and urban parts of Pakistan. For most Pakistanis Urdu is like any other language that is learnt either at school or in the mosque. Under the umbrella of Urdu there are numerous dialects that are spoken and are considered to be a separate language by those who speak the dialect. For example, the parents of all respondents in this study originated from Mirpur and speak Azad Kashmiri Punjabi. It is a spoken language and there is no written form (often confused by those outside of the community this Punjabi is different from the Sikh Punjabi and they are two separate languages). This should not mean that all Pakistanis speak the same language and it is common to hear many different languages and dialects there.

There is always external pressure on institutions like the Primary Care Trusts (PCTs) and the National Health Service to provide information in the many different ethnic languages. Of course it is important that individuals who are unable to read English have a means of obtaining that information, but this has almost become a matter of policy rather than practicality or indeed usefulness. For example for the community in question we have variety of information in Urdu, the national language of Pakistan. This supposes that all those individuals are able to read Urdu but this is not the case. Not every Pakistani can read Urdu, just as there are some White English people who may be unable to read English.

The PCTs and the National Health Service have also been under pressure to provide interpreters for those individuals who are unable to speak English. They often rely on friends and family to help them out during hospital or GP appointments, to interpret for them. Some argue that this raises issues of confidentiality for patients who do not wish to discuss their medical problems in the company of friends and family. Others are almost totally reliant on having to use friends and family for interpretation because they have no choice. This suggests that the NHS needs to do more to accommodate non-English speaking patients. Often overlooked is that these individuals often happily use friends and relatives when contacting their child's school, going to the solicitors, to the bank or when completing forms for official purposes; but how many interpreters need to be provided and by which institutions?

Some point out that some Pakistani children who enter schooling have little or no skills in English. This can place pressure on schools and teachers to help out in language tuition, but there are those who feel that it is not part of their job.

There is evidence of change, parents realizing that through speaking English they can help their children through schooling and in raising academic attainment. This does not only apply to Pakistani but to other minority ethnic groups and to White majority parents as well. Most Pakistani parents, if they are in a position to do so, will help their child to acquire English language skills before they enter schooling. Other children have to pick it up whilst at school and take longer to acquire fluency. This can have an important affect on their schooling. These children would often play 'catch up' with other White/English-speaking young people in their class. The problem is that they are not only playing 'catch up' in English but in all the other national curriculum subjects. This is inevitably reflected in their lower SATs There is a tendency to make the connection between fluency in English and raising academic standards, but this is something of which most parents are aware and work hard by teaching their children to read.

It is this 'catch-up' period that needs to be tackled. Although there are differences, most spent the early years learning their parents' language and this is true of parents who are unable to speak English. Those parents who have a grasp of the English language help their children to acquire all the skills needed to make good progress at school. Clearly more needs to be done and all the evidence from the young people suggests that most Pakistani parents would welcome further language tuition, particularly for their young people. One option would be to have pre-nursery or nursery classes that focus on teaching the English language to those pupils who require extra tuition. In this way when the child moves from nursery education to primary school they will have grasped a good knowledge of the English language. Like all initiatives there needs to be a consultation period between parents, schools and the LEA in order to examine the best way of moving forward.

Some are worried that English is being imposed on young people to the disadvantage of their native language. The vast majority of young people in this sample said they enjoy listening to English music, reading books and magazines in English and the fact that all interviews were conducted in English. This indicates that English is the preferred language of the majority of young people, a matter of choice as well as reality.

It is interesting how young people view language differently depending on who is speaking. Some point out that there is a difference between their English and the Queen's English, who in their view speaks 'proper English' (girl, age 16). Others point to a difference in American English or Scottish or Irish English. This also comes out in the popular media and the differences between broadsheet and tabloid newspapers. There are also many regional accents, for example those from Newcastle or Liverpool. The young clearly think of these as being different. As pointed out above, although they do not think of one language as being better than another, they do make distinctions between the 'different kinds' of English spoken. They have a preference for one type of English depending on where they are from. The many different accents spoken in England are also a basis for regional identity where people or communities think of themselves as being different from the next town, for example those from Lancashire and Yorkshire. Regional accents are also a way of marking out differences between groups.

Some also made the point that they do not speak formal English or 'posh' English. This was something reserved for those who went to a public school. Formal English was something to revert to during a job interview or when speaking to an individual in authority. There were many examples in the interviews of young people of Pakistani origin using a mixture of 'traditional' and English slang,

> '...and going on about *izzat* (respect) *and that*' (girl, age 15)

And again,

> '...I couldn't *hack that*' (boy, age 15)

Formal English was rarely used with friends unless of course one had attended a public school. The language of the streets for the vast majority of young people of Pakistani origin was English slang. Using slang was something to be proud of, particularly by boys who had been influenced by American gang sub-culture. They picked up slang through listening to rap music or gangsta music. On the whole girls did not approve of using English slang (although they also used it); they considered it as not speaking 'properly' or speaking English. Some intentionally spoke slang while, for others, it was not out of choice but they had missed the opportunity to learn formal or proper English while at school; but this should not be seen as unique to young Pakistanis but common to people from all backgrounds. There is clearly a hierarchy of accents and fluency in English.

Summary

The adaptability of the young includes camouflaging their tastes and their actions. It is interesting that they do not overtly rebel but they see the practised dualism in their elders. Whilst they hear the strict voices of advice on how to behave and what to avoid, they note the fact that there are numerous video shops in the community which sell and rent films. Hypocrisy was something despised by young people. At the same time they were aware it exists within their community. Boys are allowed much more freedom than girls in terms of what they can and cannot do. This is emphasized in all the peculiar cultural assumptions in which boys are allowed to socialize freely with friends after school and in the evenings, whereas girls 'must return' home after school. It was clear from the responses the unhappiness and loneliness suffered on the part of girls. The male siblings sympathized with this.

The 'bedroom culture' enjoyed by many young people and considered as being free from parental surveillance is open to inspection. It is common for parents to search the bedrooms of their young people (especially daughters) while they are at school for 'immoral' literature such as teenage magazines, which are believed by parents as having a corrupting influence on the young but which the young people consider as normal. The invasion of privacy at home was an issue that was a constant source of tension between the generations. The fear of being watched meant that many adaptive behaviours were exaggerated. This did not mean that young people simply followed instructions. They continue to act as they wish when out of sight of parents. The young people did not reflect the opinions and attitudes of parents and assume naively that young people do not have their own opinions. A change from tradition is not always considered bad, especially when it is seen as being unfair. The differences in behaviour when at home and when away from control are more exaggerated than in the rest of the community.

Despite their leisure interests most are forbidden to listen to English music and watch English films by parents. Conceding to the demands of parents and elders was common but this did not mean that they simply gave in to the wishes of parents. They made their feelings and objections clear even though it was ignored but pursued their pleasures while out of sight of parents. It is naive to assume that young people are simply 'blank slates' and that they will take on board those values without question.

The young people in the sample were clearly multilingual rather than bilingual: they could converse in many 'Asian' languages, commonly Urdu and Azad Kashmiri Punjabi as well other dialects. Languages were learnt in many different settings. Most learnt the 'home' language from parents, siblings and relatives. They also learnt languages from their peers while at school or while playing in the street. The concern is that some Pakistani children enter schooling without a grasp of the English language and this can have a detrimental effect on their schoolwork. One possible solution is to have pre-school language classes for those children who may need them.

Chapter 10

The Experience of Parents and the Biraderi

Relationships with parents

Young people often accuse their parents of not listening to them. The young people in this sample do not appear to be any different from the majority. Minor disputes can turn into bigger issues, seemingly unavoidable. This can be the start of the breakdown in communication and go on well beyond the so-called rebellious years and into adulthood. Problems in communication and breakdown occur in families of all ethnic backgrounds. For most Pakistanis there is no natural separation of the individual from his/her family and biraderi and this can have a positive or negative impact on the individual. Breakdowns in communication or relationships are put up with and persevered with. Despite the domestic situation few 'get up and leave' the family home or completely break ties. Of those who decide to leave the family home most will return to the fold sometime later. Even when the young person gets married it is customary in most biraderis, for the couple to stay with the in-laws for a period of time before they set up a home of their own. 'Letting-go' is a slow process but ties are never completely broken among the biraderi members.

This sample was typical of most; the majority of young people believed parents do not understand the needs and feelings of young people the majority of the time (87 per cent compared to 16 per cent of young people who said parents do understand them). Some gender differences were found: girls were more likely than boys to say this (85 per cent v 78 per cent respectively), but most did have a favourite parent. This can be the mother or the father. In this sample the young people often confided in another relative, usually a cousin. For the young people, particularly those who had little contact with school friends, it gave them an opportunity to talk about issues of concern or just have a chat. This does not happen with friends who are considered to be outsiders and not part of the family, unless of course they are part of the same biraderi in some other way. Friends can be seen as a potential threat to any decisions taken by the family for the young person. They are best kept out of the house and most families would not encourage a close relationship to form between their son/daughter and a friend. They are a source of emotional and confidential support for the individual. These relationships often start at school rather than through a chance meeting. They are not only a shoulder to cry on but something much more valuable during times of need. Like any group there is an inner circle of close friends (they may or may not be related).

In terms of age, the results showed that those aged 14 years were most likely to say that their parents 'understand their needs and feelings' (58 per cent). As the age of the young person increased from 15 onwards they were less likely to say their parents understand them. Those aged 16 were least likely to say that parents understand them (eight per cent). Reaching the end of compulsory schooling was a critical point for most young people as they decided what they wanted to do, or in some cases these decisions are left unwillingly to others. These were minor compared to the overall evidence, which showed that the majority believe their parents do not understand their needs and feelings. This, to some extent, reflects typical adolescent disillusionment and the desire for independence.

Issues such as freedom to choose their dress code, hairstyle, make-up, choice of a marriage partner and the freedom to continue post-16 schooling had an effect on their everyday lives. Up to a point this might be a common experience for most young people, but as we witness a breakdown in communication and the effect this would have on their future relationship with parents, we realize how important this is. The belief that parents must do much more to understand their young people was a central theme that runs throughout the sample, but they also make clear which issues need to be understood from the young person's point of view. The issues are clear as the tension between the generations become visible,

> 'Well, you can't talk about personal things, they (parents) don't understand like take arranged marriages. My cousins and friends we're given no choice. Too many but forced into' (boy, age 19)

The young people and parents appear to be at the opposite ends of the spectrum and there is no middle ground for dialogue, as this boy explains by using the word "they" and "we're" as if all parents are the same and all young people are in the same situation. It also illustrates that both boys and girls are affected.

There should be no suggestion that Pakistani parents deliberately set out to make their children's life more difficult but that is how some young people see the actions of their parents. The result for most is the complete breakdown in communication, something that both the young people and parents do not wish to see happening. This is also a period of marking out territory that neither side wishes to give up; instead both sides become more adamant. The young people put this down to the failure on the part of parents to listen. Communication was seen as being something one-sided. Parents tell their children, talk to children rather than listen to them,

> '...There's no point telling them (parents) 'cos they won't understand you, what goes on really goes on' (boy, age 19)

Again the same theme is echoed, 'there's no point telling them', but what does this include? What about the effect this will have on the young person or indeed adults who have had failed relationships? What about other concerns that affect young people, such as bullying at school? These relate to parenting skills and how different minority and majority communities relate to young people. These young people do not wish to fight with their parents over every issue or every decision, nor do they want to be in constant denial that things are not happening. It is as if parents were unable to, or did not wish to, listen to their children. Traditional norms are questioned and being eroded by young people who are challenging their parents.

There were other young people who said they got on well with their parents. They could talk to them about anything. We do have a basis for communication and understanding because these parents are interested in what their young people do; most make an effort to find out. What is lacking from the above example is the existence of real dialogue between young people and parents. For those young people who believe that parents do not understand them they would often turn to the outside, the public sphere where they see the outside and the home as two separate things,

'I can do what I want except when I go home and that I have to wear apna clothes which is so stupid!…I can't wear no make-up either' (boy, age 17)

The two separate domains are marked out, the difference between the things they cannot do at home and what they can experience outside. The young do not simply leave their tastes and preferences outside; they do not discuss them in the presence of parents and elders. Listening to parents has religious significance for some. This proved to be a dilemma that everything one's parents decide must be followed and acted upon. This could be used in a productive way, for example, encouraging the young to stay on at school and providing a moral code for the young to follow. The importance of respecting one's parents and the Islamic duty is clear,

'I respect my parents as it says in Islam. I wouldn't dare swear at them' (girl, age 16)

'Respect' is a complex notion. There are different levels, including natural reaction and the more deep-seated tension against parents. 'Respect' can mean self-assertion, or personal rights, as well as consideration for others. Beneath the surface the evidence reveals complex relationships where conflict and tension between most young people and parents are all too common. The difference between respecting parents in public but real inner feelings is not always aired in front of parents. This can lead to discontentment or when communication between the generations breaks down,

'…in front of them they do, as soon as they are out of sight they ignore them' (girl, age 17)

In this context it is argued that religion is used as a symbol of control by parents and the biraderi. For these young people a change from tradition is not considered bad, especially when they are seen as being unfair. It is naive to assume that respect from the young generation will be naturally forthcoming, even though it has religious undertones. On one level showing 'respect' to old people is a good thing. The question is what is considered to be 'good' and 'bad' and whose interpretation prevails. The young learn to keep some opinions hidden, especially when they are younger, but this invariably changes when they get older. The distinction is between respecting their parents and discussing problems, which, according to this girl, is often avoided,

'...there are problems which are simply not discussed but hidden or just avoided for a time' (girl, age 17)

This does not mean that problems avoided simply go away; quite the opposite, some young people become confrontational towards their parents,

'...I disagree with them over a lot of things which causes us to have fights which seem to go on for weeks' (girl, age 16)

The real problems remain unanswered. The young begin to feel alienated from their parents and the biraderi elders who appear to be distant from the issues facing their young people,

'They respect parents but don't agree with a lot of things they do or say, like I said forced marriages' (girl, age 19)

The underlying themes reveal the causes of tension and the attempt to keep the situation under control. Showing respect to parents is a normal part of everyday life but on the other hand, as all parents know, conflict between them and their children is inevitable when relationships break down.

Communication with parents

Most young people were unable to talk to their parents about their personal problems (85 per cent). This is perhaps the typical experience of most young people. There were particular issues highlighted. Young people felt that due to the lack of communication issues such as aspirations and marriage made them feel vulnerable but these are something that the individual may have to deal with in the future; there were more immediate issues such as bullying. Not being able to talk to parents had an enormous and immediate effect on these individuals. Being comfortable in the company of parents, where things can be openly and honestly discussed, was a sign of good parenting. Like all young people this was treasured and something to boast about in front of their friends. Inevitably parents have to try harder than their children to create an atmosphere of understanding and trust. In reality sometimes this was not achieved and the young people made this clear and public.

As pointed out earlier, for most young people of Pakistani origin their first language is English, whereas for many older parents it is their native language, i.e. Punjabi or Urdu. This is not a result of speaking different languages but the lack of the understanding about their lives. It was not a language problem but a more general communication problem. Young people aged 14 was most likely to say that they can talk to their parents about their personal problems (46 per cent). Most 14-year-olds echoed the following point,

'They do when you're young but when you get older like 14, 15 they don't' (girl, age 16)

Again slight gender differences were found: boys were more likely than girls to 'talk to their parents about their personal problems' (15 per cent v 13 per cent), a small finding which does point to the particular difficulties for girls. This may be a general trend for most young people. Age was an important variable in most issues. The younger the age of the respondent the more likely they were to listen to their parents without posing a challenge to the decision of their parents. As they grow older they wish to decide for themselves over a whole range of issues, but for those who do not get their way they begin to feel ignored. What was striking was that very few young people said that they have a good relationship with their parents, where they are free to air their opinions. It was something that only a small number pointed out. One exception was,

'I can talk to my parents. I can even disagree with them' (boy, age 18)

The experiences of White/English children include rebellion and disagreement, if not to this extent. There are many young people who may feel that they are unable to talk to their parents about anything private and personal, but the young Pakistanis feel they are pressured to do things and to follow expectations often of a different kind. In many respects the experiences of Pakistani young people are essentially different, especially in terms of the freedom given to boys and girls. This suggests there has not only been change among the new generation but growing tensions. We now witness constant conflict and the reporting of feelings of alienation and estrangement. To some extent this is assumed to be a normal part of growing up (although there seems to be little research evidence to support the assertion generally). Most constantly referred to the lack of understanding on the part of their parents and the how rules are applied differently to girls and boys,

'I don't want a lot just the same like go out with my girlfriends in the evenings and the weekends or play sports with them' (girl, age 16)

Of course not all girls were discontented with their parents over the issue of 'freedom'. Some girls enjoyed enormous freedom to do the things that they wished to do, including going out with friends (and relatives) in the evening, playing sports, going to the cinema, eating out, going on holiday or excursions. This also had an effect on their relationships in terms of communication and most said they could discuss personal problems with their parents, particularly the mother. However, most girls who were not in this position would compare their level of freedom with that of their brothers and male cousins,

'...like marriage, not giving the same freedom as my brothers' (ibid)

Getting away with things often meant that parents turn a blind eye to the behaviour of boys; the girls point out,

'Boys always get away with a lot more than girls' (girl, age 17)

The girl makes it clear that young people enjoy some freedom when they are younger but this is taken away when they reach teenage years. She would like to achieve the same things and be given the same amount of freedom as her brother. It is important to remember that girls often compared their experiences to their brother(s). This adds to their sense of resentment. The lack of choice available to them was clear and so is being nurtured to behave in a specific way but one that is in contradiction to their everyday experience. The beliefs of parents and the biraderi are instilled in the young to behave in a particular way,

'...like girls to leave school at 16 and stay at home...You know the situation girls get forced to do a lot of thing which they don't want to like get married especially from Pakistan' (girl, age 17)

Understanding is not just about being allowed to wear what one pleases but about all things that are personal and private such as choosing one's marriage partner, but most only hope that marriage will be delayed until after post-compulsory schooling,

'...Oh and also I want to study and not get married. They don't understand, I have to say that' (girl, age 16)

Boys would 'get away' with things that girls would be reprimanded for by the parents. For the boys they would test their parents in terms of whether they would give into their demands. For example, whether they could stay out or watch television late into the night while the sisters would stay in. It is not only the parents that uphold codes of behaviour but also the relatives, as another young person pointed out. The biraderi reinforces its values on the young,

'...as you know boy and girls are treated differently by parents, ras-thar-dar (relatives)' (girl, age 16)

Many girls said their parents do not allow them to wear Western style clothes, instead preferring them to wear shalwar and kameez both at home and outside. Clearly personal will wins over the authority of parents, if secretly so. One mentioned that girls 'get changed outside'. The freedom to choose what they want to wear is one issue that causes tension in the home and at the same time girls were aware that boys have that freedom. This girl was typical of others,

'My parents especially my father doesn't like the way I dress. I like to wear tight clothes they don't like it. I can wear what I want at school like trousers (girl, age 16)

She also realizes that she may be seen by relatives wearing something quite different, which will be reported back to her parents. The constant worry about being seen and her parents finding out play on her mind. This is another example of the two worlds in which most young people live, particularly the girls. The ideal situation would be no longer to hide her preferences,

> 'The ideal situation would be for girls to go from home to school wearing what they want and not get changed outside and worry about family and relatives seeing them' (ibid)

Dressing modestly is part of an Islamic and cultural heritage, but this invariably varies among Muslims. In some Muslim communities the women are expected to be in purdah while in others, however, some adaptation has occurred. The girls wanted equality similar to their brothers in terms of dress,

> 'I would like to wear what I wear to school at home' (girl, age 17)

Again, although realizing that things 'should be equal' they are at the same aware that boys and girls are treated differently.

> 'It should be equal for boys and girls but it isn't' (girl, age 16)

This should not mean that all boys could wear what they please. Some, especially the younger ones, were forbidden to wear jeans because their parents thought it made them look 'scruffy' and 'untidy' and does not create a respectable image. Dressing differently outside of the home had its consequences if found out, but despite the possible disapproval the girls were willing to dress as they pleased,

> '…and then get killed by my dad!' (girl, age 17)

There is a desire to be open with parents rather to hide feelings. The girls want to be open with their parents and 'not get changed outside' but at the same time many realize that it is unrealistic. It is as if the real feelings are hidden and not openly discussed where they can be open to criticism from parents. It is interesting to remark that boys were aware of their sisters' situation at home, especially when they wish to enjoy similar levels of freedoms as them. They often sympathized with their sisters, but at the same time they realize there is little they can do to help.

Where rules are seen as being unfair the young people were quick to point this out to their parents even though many accepted that their opinions would be ignored. The clash between choice and imposition is clear and so are outcomes in terms of the breakdown in relationships. This is an outcome that is not intended, at least by the girls. A good relationship can be had with parents if only certain attitudes would change; indeed if only they would adapt their lives more openly and honestly both to the prevailing culture and to the real tenets of Islam.

It is perhaps a naive assumption that people simply follow rules without question. What is viewed as being over harsh and strict was always challenged. They have their own battles with parents, some of which they win while others are lost. It is worth noting that whilst mothers are generally more conservative and traditional, as discussed earlier, it is the father, for all his greater experience, who is forced into the position of authoritarianism by the expectations of the biraderi. The more obvious reasons for discontent were highlighted,

'I think that as I am getting older I am arguing more with them (parents) about everything, like the way I dress, the way I look like make-up' (girl, age 16)

The underlying problems are ones of being 'ignored' and considered as being 'stupid' because of one's gender has an enormous effect on the individual. Culture is considered as being more restrictive than Islam. The girls attempt to enforce their rights to be treated as equals in terms of intellect and available opportunities but the reality for some can be different, as this girl explains,

'Girls are treated as being stupid who only want to wear make-up. I think that's just an excuse for men to ignore us and I think Islam is used wrongly to deny females a lot of opportunities' (girl, age 16)

The crucial issue was the lack of understanding on the part of parents, and the general restrictions placed on girls,

'It has to be understanding and giving young people freedom and choice. Like I said earlier with them like going out I mean I can't except with my brothers and sister. I get frustrated angry... I think most Pakistani parents have driven young boys and girls away from them' (girl, age 17)

The pressure faced by many young people (mainly boys) to do well and to succeed was also highlighted. This is based on the izzat devised by parents but to a lesser extent on the need for izzat for the individual. This pressure for prestige is felt the more strongly because the parents care so much about it. They will their sons to be successful.

'Young kids are under so much pressure these days, like to do well in exams, get a job and everything. But I think it's so much worse in apna houses, you always get compared with cousins and relatives to do well at school, go to university and become a hotshot lawyer, there's added pressure' (boy, age 17)

The relationship between parents and young people may not all be one-sided in favour of parents and elders. This young man continued by saying,

'A lot of parents are probably secretly scared now they know if their children really stood up for themselves they'll lose and they know it. At the end of the day parents need their children then kids needing their parents and relatives' (ibid)

In this study not one young person mentioned that despite all the tension within the household leaving home is an alternative for them. Although not directly discussed, young people know this was an unrealistic option in the family. This suggests the cultural stranglehold parents and biraderi have over young people.

Issues of control

Young people believe their parents have the final say on many issues. The young people did not resist control but like all they were resisting excessive control. This is not the parents view, they want to protect their children from possible dangers; staying out till late was something that was likely to endanger their children, especially the girls, and thus they would restrict their movement. Control was something parents desired to have over their young,

'…you can see in people's houses, like my relative's homes, there are arguments between young people and parents' (boy, age 19)

The need to exercise control on the part of parents is clear yet, at the same time, resisted as a principle in allowing choice. There is also a fear on the part of parents, who are worried about the reaction of the wider biraderi and the accusation of failing to control their sons and especially daughters,

'…but parents don't broadcast it in public their arguments, because it will be base-thi (shame) in front of all the biraderi, you know the relatives they'll accuse your parents of not being able to control their own children. So they're forcing young people to do things' (boy, age 19)

Labelling plays an important role within this community as well as the sanctions that are imposed on parents and young people. Like labelling, 'gossip' is frequently used as a deterrent within the community. Both relatives and parents act as higher authorities,

'We get told off not only from our parents but also from all the other relatives' (ibid)

Where the home is seen as a place of control and hidden feelings, the 'outside' is seen as being free from parental surveillance but also a place where boys and girls enjoy equally a certain amount of freedom,

'…but outside girls and boys do what they want to' (girl, age 17)

Although parents clearly exercise enormous control over young people, the situation is changing as more and more young people are challenging the authority of their parents,

'…young people are doing everything, even girls, even if they're married. Parents think they have control, on the whole young people have it much more than parents actually think, most know it's true' (girl, age 19)

There are many signs of change and this is also an example of a breakdown of communication between the generations,

'Young people like my relatives and friends, including the girls are listening less and less to their parents' (boy, age 19)

Control is rarely accepted despite the consequences,

'Kids are deciding to sort their lives out instead of being told or being pushed into. I think that as young people are getting older they have a lot more freedom than when they are younger' (boy, age 14)

It is a naive assumption that the older generation has some kind of control over the thoughts and actions of their offspring. The very assertion of confident 'control' spells trouble. To a point some young people have lost some respect for their parents and elders. It suggests a major cultural shift in attitudes from those taken for granted in the traditional community. Respect of parents and elders is always a problem in Western cultures. Young people want to respect their elders and wish to earn respect in their own turn but there is a peculiar barrier of hypocrisy in the Pakistani community. This is important since young people recognized that respecting parents and elders has religious significance. This very pressure to demonstrate respect, in terms of behaviour, makes it all the more different.

The Biraderi

Pakistanis are often grouped together for research purposes and referred to as the 'Pakistani community' but underneath there are many biraderis and sub-biraderis. Each biraderi and sub-biraderi has its own norms, values and traditions. The larger biraderis can comprise of five hundred families whereas others can be much smaller, say fifty families. There are also the many sects, sub-sects, castes and sub-castes that add to the overall complex picture. A definition of the biraderi is difficult since members can be blood relatives who can be easily traceable or they can simply be fellow countrymen/women who originated from a particular part of Pakistan. It can be as broad as anyone who is considered to be 'part of the family' and this category is much more difficult to define. Members can also be from different sects and castes and each biraderi is different, and so is its composition. The traditions have an important influence on its members, for example, whether the young person will be encouraged to stay on at school or leave.

The biraderi is a close self-contained unit, which was a characteristic of the early immigrants, but evidence suggests that it is showing signs of falling apart into smaller family units along the lines of the nuclear family, where help is offered to immediate family members rather than to the larger biraderi. Of course not all biraderi members can be loaned money but there was a time in the early settlement period where this was perhaps true. The sense of obligation of many in this community is changing.

The young people are simply pointing out the change from when they were young. The common stereotypical view that the biraderi 'looks after its own' has never been true. Like in all societies the affluent members of the biraderi can access all types of services, while others who have little influence or status find it difficult.

The one occasion where most members of the biraderi congregate is during wedding celebrations. Unlike most English weddings, where a few select family and friends would be invited, most Pakistani weddings are on a grand scale: inviting two thousand guests for the celebrations is not uncommon. For those families who can afford to do this it is seen as a symbol of their wealth and status in the biraderi. It is also a chance to increase the family's izzat and to become accepted as one of the more affluent families. Those who have the financial resources hold such celebrations both in Pakistan and in the UK to allow for all relatives to take part. Most young people made references to the function of the biraderi and how it is changing,

'I think families are looking after their own children instead of lending a lot of money to their brothers and sisters and relatives, especially now when a lot of people like my relatives are unemployed' (boy, age 19)

The biraderi is similar to being part of a club or like belonging to an exclusive members' club. Most members of the biraderi live in self-enclosed units and socialize little with 'outsiders', even though the outsiders are part of the larger 'Pakistani community'. Clearly not every family is accepted as being equal or considered as 'part of the club', and having access to money is reflected in one's status within the biraderi, perhaps as opposed to having qualifications,

'If you do well everyone looks up to you and if you don't no one talks to you especially if you haven't got any money, none of the relatives want to know you…ras-thar-dar (relatives) only want to know you if you do well' (boy, age 18)

For many Pakistanis poverty and financial hardship endured in Pakistan determined the close relationship between family members. The reliance upon each other and the family has a continuing influence in Britain. It is largely an economic relationship between individuals in terms of what could be offered to fellow biraderi members. Like in Pakistan the visiting homes of relatives is an important feature of communal life in Britain. The reason is to do with financial insecurity, where the majority of rural families have little if any savings and have to rely on the biraderi in times of need, which can be daily reliance and is often in the form of hand-outs from biraderi members.

Most young people said they visit homes of relatives (seventy-nine per cent) with their parents as opposed to going out to the cinema or just going out as a family (eleven per cent) with their parents,

'My parents say they're (relatives) really important and the family should come first. Sometimes I don't want to go to my relatives but my parents force me to go' (boy, age 14)

For the majority of older Pakistani people visiting relatives is an integral part of communal life, to maintain close ties with relatives and friends, but this does not appear to be the same for the young people. Visiting homes of relatives was an activity done with parents; they would not do so alone. In some situations the young people would go alone to their uncle or aunt's house, not to see elders but to talk to their cousin of a similar age about something personal or just for a general chat. The girls found making friends with cousins easier (simply because most are allowed to do so by parents) than forming friendships with non-relatives. Parents saw these relationships as something good because it brought the respective families closer.

Visiting relatives can be done at any time of the day. As many older Pakistanis tend to live near other biraderi members, women in particular will go round for a chat. If this is during the day they will often go alone but in the evening it is common to take their husband and some of the children, especially the younger ones. The length of the stay is dependent on a number of factors, such as what day it is. During school terms they will often leave the house by 7 o'clock. If someone is unwell this might mean having to stay the night but some point out that this can be done out of public obligation rather than individual choice.

The frequency and time spent at the home of a relative also depends on the circumstance. For example, if someone has died then most close relatives will stay for several nights, or at least until the funeral has taken place. It would be the job of the close relatives (usually the boys) to make arrangements, for example, for contacting relatives both here in the UK and also in Pakistan, informing relatives of the death; arranging the catering; the sleeping arrangements and all the funeral arrangements, depending on whether the body is to be buried in the UK or taken to Pakistan for burial. The close relatives are given a task, whether it is looking after the men or women guests or arranging paperwork such as visas. It is obligatory for all close relatives to offer help and support to the family of the deceased. Similar activity will take place in Pakistan, except that in most cases it would be on a much larger scale, especially if there are surviving close relatives in Pakistan. With many more people coming to do 'whas-sawce' (condolences); the whas-sawce period normally lasts for forty days and a special meal (Khatum) is served after the fourth, fifteenth, thirty-fifth or after the fortieth, but this practice varies considerably among Pakistanis in Bradford. In this way the biraderi is seen by many, especially the older Pakistanis, as being supportive.

Where parents see relatives as being security in times of need, some young people see this differently. A change from tradition is not always seen as being bad, especially where young people view it as being perhaps outdated. Parents believe it is their duty to take their offspring to the homes of relatives who are in a position to transmit the norms of the community. Often young people are praised for visiting and keeping in touch with relatives and such young people are treated as changa bacha (good children) and izzi-thi nay bacha (obedient children). Obedience and loyalty to parents and elders is expected. On the surface the extended family is seen as being supportive both emotionally and financially. Beneath the surface young people believe the extended family is viewed as a controlling institution. It is clear that by remaining in the biraderi the advantages are obvious. The help offered is emotional,

'Like my cousins, uncles come over to our house if my mum and dad is sick or if like when my granddad died everyone came over' (boy, age 15)

and also financial,

'Well they give you money if you need it. We did when we bought a house for lodgers and we needed some money my mum went to this house and she got it the same day!' (boy, age 15)

Offering help to relatives has both advantages and disadvantages: on the one hand relatives and family members offered support to each other like childminding, but on the other hand there is an issue of privacy. Relatives living in close proximity can be under surveillance from others. Those who wanted privacy from relatives became difficult to maintain. For example those living nearby were often aware of who is visiting a particular house or is invited for dinner. For many older parents this is normal and a sign of closeness of relatives, but some young people find this difficult to understand. For them maintaining privacy in their private lives was seen as paramount. This does not mean that they strongly disliked relatives visiting but they wanted prior notice of who would be visiting.

Living nearby did not mean that relatives 'got on' with each other; as in all communities disputes with relatives was common. Disputes with friends were not something to be concerned about since they were not part of the inner circle of support and biraderi-hood, but quarrels with relatives were something quite different. The young people were aware of 'who is not talking to who?' and 'why'? Since most would be related it would be difficult for individuals or families to avoid each other, for example at a wedding or a funeral. Close relatives often help to build bridges and encourage communication.

Relationships with elders

The 'elders' play an important role in the life of the Pakistani community in the United Kingdom. They serve hundreds of distinct and separate communities and often act as the main link with the wider society. Older Pakistanis generally bestow enormous respect to elders as they had done in Pakistan. For most young people the idea of external elders is an alien concept, for example in White/English communities. The issue for most young people is that they are unclear as to the purpose or the role of the traditional elders. Instead in most cases the young pick out the negative aspects of or in the behaviour of elders.

Most young people find it difficult to relate to elders in any meaningful way. This is not just a generational difference but based on different lifestyles, attitudes and experiences. The 'elders' are symbolic of the past. Most young people (92 per cent) believe 'Pakistani' elders do not understand the needs and the feelings of young people in Bradford, whereas only eight per cent said Pakistani elders understand the needs and feelings of young people. Both boys and girls were equally likely to express this (91 per cent v 92 per cent respectively). Issues of freedom and independence and the preference for cultural values are some of the areas where elders do not understand young people. A typical example,

> 'Girls have more freedom than our mothers did but things haven't changed as much as young people would like them to change' (girl, age 16)

Like many she is very clear where the change needs to come,

> '...parents and Mulvis (religious leaders) need to change' (girl, age 16)

This highlights the gap between young people and elders but also between parents and their young; the relationship is unequal but also where parents and Mulvis are considered as being on the 'other side'. Some argued there is a 'barrier' between parents and young people which is the result of lack of communication between generations,

> 'I think there is a barrier between parents and young people...you know parents never talk to their kids and the kids never bother' (boy, age 19)

But despite a lack of respect shown to elders they continue to play an important role within the community, influencing parents to keep their sons and daughters under strict control and maintaining the status quo, namely the beliefs and the values of the community. Where they believe rules have been broken criticism is both open and hostile. One young person used the word 'hypocrites',

> 'Most of my friends accuse them of being hypocrites' (girl, age 16)

The distinction between what Islam says to Pakistanis and the individual's action suggests a different type of behaviour,

> '...Pakistani elders just preach what it says in Islam. People know they are the ones just saying that because it makes them feel good' (girl, age 17)

The 'blame' is placed on the 'other' culture, i.e. British,

> 'They blame everything on young people, especially the bad influences of Britain and White girls' (girl, age 17)

The existence of a cultural enemy means the blame lies on 'them', i.e. Britain. This displaces the faults in their own behaviour and attitudes. Young people display their resentment towards parents and elders and argue their point, but much of this is kept secret since it is in their own interests. This also reveals contradictions where the freedom-seeking young people are viewed as being wayward and corrupted and who have taken on kufr attitudes. Some elders are clearly allowed 'to get away with it' simply because they are in authority. It is these individuals that are picked out. It is important to remember the enormous power still held by Muslim religious leaders in contrast to religious leaders in Western societies.

Summary

Pakistanis are part of a complex community with divisions based on age, gender, caste and sect. There are also many sub-castes and sub-sects that continue to exist as they had in Pakistan. This is nothing new where the Pakistanis form part of large extended communities (the biraderi), something that existed earlier in Europe but which has to some extent been succeeded. Nepotism, as in most communities, plays an important part in deciding which families will have access to goods and services, for example the purchase of houses and property while an individual is unemployed. The general long-held stereotype of Pakistanis is that they are part of a supportive culture and one that provides limitless physical, emotional and financial help. There are wide variations: some have access to all the services and help available in the community while others make do with help from family members only.

Labelling plays a significant part where traditional attitudes are maintained between different religious sects. The biraderi is also in a position to socially exclude families who have been labelled as 'bad' and who have little social standing within the community. The pressure placed on young people comes from the biraderi and parents are often seen as simply following those values. Young people are under enormous pressure to conform to the wishes of the biraderi, for example in arranged marriages, which young people believe are outdated. The failure on the part of parents to listen to young people is a cause of tension and conflict and is common in the majority of Pakistani households.

Chapter 11

Institutionalized Racism?
Gangs and Ethnic Minorities[1]

Despite the media coverage and the growing interest in 'gangs' there is little empirical literature on gangs in the UK and even fewer on gangs from minority ethnic communities, particularly those from the Pakistani community. The disturbances in Bradford in 1995, and more recently in 2001, point to street gang formation among young Pakistanis, which are diverse in their nature and in activities. The necessity to be sensitive when dealing with minority ethnic communities in relation to crime partly explains the limited research.

What we know about 'gangs' is that they are based on age, gender and race, but this information tends to derive from America. There is little empirical evidence in the British context and in particular on 'Pakistani gangs' in the UK. This is despite media coverage surrounding the disturbances in Bradford in 1995 and in 2001 as well as in Burnley and Oldham. One problem is gaining access to young people who are willing to talk about 'gangs' (and not just those who are active gang members) in their neighbourhood and the effect this has on their and the wider community. The necessity to be culturally sensitive when dealing with minority ethnic communities when examining crime and criminal activity partly explains the limited research into this area. Those individuals (and communities) involved carefully hide some matters, since it is in their interest to do so. Outsiders are sometimes forced to ignore these matters since any attempt to uncover the truth would bring accusations of racism. All this research describes the incidence of gangs, new definitions of minority culture; influences and reactions from the gangs themselves to the elders and the police; yet less is known about the causes of gangs, the influences on their formation and the cultures they exhibit.

The young people sampled talked about their community and the local neighbourhood, with particular emphasis on gangs. For most Pakistani parents the Mirpuri culture prevailed and determined their position in the community both before and after immigration to the United Kingdom. One recurring theme that comes out strongly from the empirical evidence is that the 'culture' of most young Pakistanis is largely similar to their White/English counterparts and this is often in conflict with their biraderi or home life (Din, 2001). It is as if the young people in this community

---

1   A shorter version of this chapter was adapted for a Journal paper: Din, I. and Cullingford, C. (2005) 'Pakistani Gangs in Schools', *Race Equality Teaching*, Vol.24, No.1, pp. 16-19, Autumn.

live in a different world to their parents. For these young people the 'British culture' is not an alien culture but one which is their own. The Pakistani sub-culture or gangs has arisen partly in response to this and the other external issues facing young people generally.

The existence of sub-cultures is not a new phenomenon and some have received enormous media attention, such as punks, mods or rockers. Research on the sub-culture of gangs in the British context is limited. Some references have been made to a male Pakistani sub-culture in the formation of 'gangs' (*Bradford Commission report*, 1996). What was crucially overlooked before the 1995 riots in Bradford was the existence and the involvement of gangs. The empirical evidence presented reveals the emergence of the Pakistani gangs not only in Bradford. Like others, it emerged with its own unique identity and purposes. The evidence also points to the formation of gangs within gangs, whilst maintaining a common identity with the larger gang they have their own unique values and behaviours. Some members of gangs revel in the idea that they are part of a 'gang', whereas others would discreetly admit to just hanging about with mates or in 'groups' and not want to be labelled as being part of a 'gang' or, worse, a criminal gang.

While there is much literature on 'Black youth culture' this has not been followed up with equal curiosity on 'Asian' youth cultures (Gilroy, 1987; McRobbie, 1991; Sharma et al, 1996). Since historically, 'Asians' have often been in British research on ethnic minorities and gangs (Goodey, 2001). There are notable exceptions, Wardak (1994), who looked at Pakistani gangs in Scotland; Webster (1997) and Clare Alexander's work on the 'Asian gang' (2001), who suggests gangs are an ongoing process in the criminalization of Asian youth. Alexander's work explored youth cultures and identity are all examples of gang research. The study was based at a youth project which catered for Asian young men in south London; all the men interviewed where of Bangladeshi Muslim origin. It explored the 'gang' activity of these young men and the labels which were placed on them by schools and the police.

Historically 'Asians' do not appear to pose the same problems as sections of the Black population (Fitzgerald, 1995). Although there is literature on 'Black youth culture' this has not been followed up with equal curiosity on 'Asian' (or on Pakistani) youth cultures (Gilroy, 1987; McRobbie, 1991; Sharma et al, 1996). More recently the problem of youth gangs on British streets has been the target of much recent media attention (Education Guardian, 2004; BBC News, 2005; Britten, 2005).

'Asian' gangs

'Asians' are often an overlooked group in British research on ethnic minorities and gangs (Goodey, 2001), despite the evidence that shows gangs tend to be formed within groups of recent immigrants (Curry and Decker, 1998). However, notable exceptions are Wardak (1994), who looked at Pakistani gangs in Scotland, and Webster (1997), who suggests gangs are an ongoing process in the criminalization of Asian youth.

Asians do not appear to pose the same problems as sections of the Black population (Fitzgerald, 1995), research tends to 'de-homogenize' the category 'Asian' and the variations between and within the different Asian categories (Goodey, 2001).

There has been some attempt to examine the link between ethnic minorities in Britain and crime (Smith, 1994; Fitzgerald, 1995). Historically 'Asians' tend to be depicted as victims of crime, often of racial harassment, (see Hesse et al, 1992; Connolly, 1998; Percy, 1998), rather than perpetrators. Black youngsters responded to a racist and hostile society by generating sub-cultural formations that have given a sense of collective solidarity (Osgerby, 1998). Brake (1985) commented that the stereotypical image of the 'passive' Asian has been replaced by militancy in the light of racial attacks in East London. Similarly, Goodey (2001) reports the shift from 'passive' to 'aggressive' behaviour of Asians. For example, the Scarman report into the 1981 Brixton disorders noted that some Asian youths were also in confrontation with the police during that period and more recently during the 2001 disturbances in a number of northern towns. There is also a visible increase of Asian youth in the criminal justice system (Spalek and Wilson, 2002). Earlier studies indicated that crime was likely to be curtailed because of the nature of the Muslim culture (Batta et al, 1978; Mawby and Batta, 1980), however our findings do not suggest that this is still applicable to the new generation of British-born Pakistanis.

Some point to the causes of the riots as a result of integration into the wider British society (Parekh report, 2000). For some there are broader issues of social exclusion and discrimination as it affects minority ethnic groups in Europe (Madanipour et al, 1998). Some have pointed out that as a result of social exclusion this is linked to criminalization of some minority ethnic groups (see Schokkenbroek, 1994; Goodey, 2000). This situation has been made worse because of the negative references to Islam such as during the Gulf war (Goodey, 2001), where Islam and Islamophobia is seen as the new threat to the West (Khanum, 1992; Favell and Tambini, 1995; Runneymede Trust, 1997; Allen, 2003), and the association of 'Muslims' in general with terrorism since 9/11. This suggests that authorities like the police and the criminal justice system intentionally discriminate against Asians or Muslims through their everyday dealings.

Attention has gradually changed from the general focus on 'gangs' to particular types of gang-related behaviour, more specifically Pakistani gangs. The *Bradford Commission report* (1996) points to the large amount of time spent on the street by young men and the increasing attractiveness to 'gangsta' fashion along the lines of American youth gangs. Khan (1997) describes this as the new 'street culture' and their activities such as drug dealing, violent crime and prostitution (see also Macey, 1999a; Macey, 1999b). Similarly, Bhatti (1999) found that the majority of Asian boys stood around on street corners and talked, but also found that some boys were 'interested in cars' but had not been caught; and there was also a high incidence of drug abuse among Asian boys.

Macey (1999b) describes harassment and violence in public and private spheres perpetrated by young Pakistani men on their own community, for example on family members, wives or daughters (see also Shaw, 1994; Patel, 1994; Alibhai-Brown,

1998; Piper, 1998). The 'mobile phone mob' described by Macey is a result of some offence on religious (or moral) grounds or the concerns over behaviour/dress (Afshar, 1994; Kassam, 1997).

There has been a noticeable influence of Black culture on young Asians/ Pakistanis. For example, Scott Fleming in his study based in a secondary school in North London found that some British-born Asians have become part of a much larger multi-ethnic street gang that is heavily influenced by Caribbean youth street culture. This could be seen through dress code that forms part of a 'uniform' of the street: it includes loose-fitting shirt, baggy jeans, a ski-jacket, running shoes and a personal stereo (Jarvie, 1991; Bhatti, 1999). Or listening to Black rap music, which is a favourite pastime of some young Pakistanis (Din and Cullingford, 2004).

Riots or 'race riots'

A good starting point for the examination of gangs in Bradford is the riots that occurred in the city in summer of 1995 and also in 2001. The riots of 1995 in Bradford were still fresh in the minds of most young people who were interviewed and they made reference to those events; who was responsible? And what were the 'trigger' issues? All the young people sampled thought the riots were a 'bad thing', not just for Bradford itself but also for the Pakistani/Muslim community. The young people interviewed were not totally surprised that the riots had occurred, but at the same time most were fearful that the whole Pakistani community would be tarnished. They were apprehensive about the situation and about what would happen in the future. For example, potential employers may note the postcode when young people are applying for jobs or even when applying for a university or college place. They were aware of labelling and how it can affect both individuals and communities, especially minority communities which they are part of.

On one level some of the more obvious reasons for the riots were mentioned, such as unemployment and the lack of money. This was something that they noted; common issues affecting many inner-city areas and the effect this can have on the community's sense of insecurity and helplessness.

> 'Well, a lot of things like unemployment, no jobs, no money, boys just dossing about, poverty in the area' (girl, age 16)

> 'Many of the lads are unemployed they say there isn't much to do and they say they don't have much money' (boy, age 16)

These young people were aware of the many issues affecting their community, in particular the lack of employment, something that was available in abundance in the 1950s and the 1960s in the textile industry. The closing down of factories had a psychological effect on the community as a whole. The disappearance of old jobs had not been replaced by newer forms of employment such as white-collar work on any scale. This was something that they almost expected would happen in the redevelopment of the region.

This is something that we have seen in other parts of the country. The lack of jobs is particularly striking where traditional jobs have been lost, such as those in the mining community and in the steel industry. The difficulties faced to regenerate those areas, to attract investment and jobs, are well known. Those areas that suffered from riots have to try considerably harder to repair the damage, to encourage businesses to locate or even to stay. People had already noticed the lack of suitable employment, and the riots made things more difficult.

The Manningham area of Bradford has long being labelled as a high crime area by many people who live and work there, but it was not just crime that these young people pointed out but particular kinds of crime, such as drugs and gangs which are much more difficult to get rid of once they take hold in the community. In this way crime affects everyone, with the increased desire for some families to move out of a certain area, even if it is to another part of the city,

'We used to live in Manningham on L. a few years ago but we moved, my father said that there was too much crime and drugs and gangs' (boy, age 18)

In this case it is the young person who reports to his parents about lads hanging around street corners and his parents reacted by moving elsewhere. It is the 'hanging around' that created a certain uneasiness and fear among the general public rather than any actual crime perpetrated. It is the fear of crime that most people worry about. In the following case it eventually led to the boy's family moving to another part of Bradford,

'I used to see Pakistani lads in groups just hanging around street corners which my father and mother didn't like' (boy, age 18)

This was a theme that was reiterated frequently, the desire to move out of certain areas and the connection with young lads hanging about on the street,

'My cousins got beaten by the lads on the corner of B Street my uncle said he'd move. They just want to know that they run this street. You can't tell them off because they will come and break your windows or break your car' (girl, age 14)

Moving to another part of Bradford did not necessarily mean that they would be free from the gang-related activities but there was less of it. These young people make the point that most areas of Bradford are affected. Like many others in the sample they did not want to be brushed with the same stroke as 'one of them'. This boy wanted to do well at school and go to university and his family did not want him to get mixed in with the 'wrong crowd' and this was a reason for the whole family moving to another part of Bradford. These areas of Bradford have traditionally been the focus of high rates of unemployment. This has an adverse effect on housing, which means that most families and individuals do not have the opportunity to move out of 'sink areas' or 'sink communities'.

On another level this demonstrates how families, given the resources, make decisions as to where to live. Crime can affect residents and push families out of the district when they may not want to move. Taking into account that many Pakistanis live near other family or relatives this has an effect of taking apart traditional communities or the biraderi. It also goes against much traditional thinking that only White people desire to move out of Asian areas (commonly known as the 'White flight'). Some argue that this is based on racial grounds and that White people do not wish to reside in Asian areas. Underneath is the desire for all people, irrespective of ethnic background, to move out of 'sink areas'. They all want to move out of undesirable high-crime areas. This is 'Pakistani flight'. It is not a new phenomenon but one that has been happening for a long time.

The effects of gangs operating in the community are pronounced. Most parents realize that in such neighbourhoods it is difficult if not impossible to stay clear of the activities of gangs and the fear of the effect this will have on them and their siblings. The community elders (as well parents) play a crucial part in helping young men to stay away from crime and gangs and again the recurring theme of having an association with the 'wrong crowd',

> 'There needs something to be done boys especially can get mixed in with the wrong crowd. This is a reality for most parents.' (girl, age 14)

This is a worry for all parents, but given the social environment in which they live, parents and young people are aware that this is a distinct possibility. Striking a friendship at school or simply through playing football in the street can lead to forming friendships of the 'wrong' kind. It becomes difficult to stay anonymous in the neighbourhood where some people make the effort to get to know others and what they do, for their own purposes. Many young people are seen congregating in the evening or at the weekend, supposedly 'doing nothing' except talking and socializing. This is a favourite pastime of some. The problem is that groups of young people are not easily separable as being law-abiding or those that take part in criminal activities. They often get brushed with the same label as being 'yobs'. This makes the job of detecting gang members much more difficult. They draw very little attention to themselves and are not distinguishable in terms of dress. While other gang members can be identifiable through their dress code, hairstyle or a symbol such as a tattoo, they want to be recognizably different from the next gang.

Most of the gangs are territorial; they have their own 'turf'. It is their neighbourhood and they set their own rules and rites of passage. Trespassing onto another's neighbourhood is strictly forbidden and illegal dealings on another's turf can lead to a gang war. Much of it is open and public and little is hidden in terms of their activities. In this sense the gang members take control of the neighbourhood. They want to know what is happening on their turf and who is doing what. The gangs are part of the community and a reality for most. Local gangs are fighting for their own 'turf' or territory in order to take control of the drugs trade and conduct other illegal activities.

Other young people in the sample made the distinction between the law-abiding and those who congregate for criminal purposes. In fact they look like 'ordinary' young people. This also shows that many areas of Bradford are prone to young people 'hanging about'; appearing to be 'doing nothing', at least on first impressions. It is this first impression that counts and one that labels an area with a certain kind of title. On another level it labels individuals and their communities, which is much harder to shake off,

'You see them near S..., M... where the riots took place' (boy, age 19)

'I cross the road when I see them on L. they hang about in small gangs so they don't get in trouble by the police. They'll pretend to be talking, hanging about but really they want to know who's doing what and what the next gang is doing' (boy, age 16).

The lack of recreational facilities or community centres, where young people can meet up with friends and take part in activities, was also highlighted. Parents often point out the lack of facilities or centres that young people can attend in the evenings. Community centres can play a crucial part in the lives of young men and women. They can be a source of help and support in terms of providing advice on issues such as benefits, housing, education and employment. Those who work in the centres can be seen as role models for the young people who attend. The young can see them as a reference point for all types of help. It is also a valuable opportunity to do youth work promoting the issues surrounding non-participation in education and employment. Equally they can help build (or strengthen) bridges between majority and minority communities. They are in a position to do outreach work, and are in a prime position to understand the needs of the communities they serve.

There are other young people on the streets for a whole different purpose and intention. They want to be on the 'streets' for all the wrong reasons. This should not be put down to 'yobbish' or 'laddish' behaviour since many areas are affected, but is the activity of organized street gangs,

'It's all to do with drugs and stealing cars, burning them, like torching and claiming insurance, it's big business' (boy, age 19)

'They're gangs of boys going round committing small crime like stealing cars and selling drugs. They can do what they want' (girl, age 19)

The police have an important role to play in the local community,

'The police should be more stricter, get tough on these lads because they think they can do anything they want but the parents also have a responsibility they should also make an effort' (girl, age 17)

The joint 'responsibility', or a partnership between the police and parents, is seen as a way of tackling many of the crimes committed. Many of the problems pointed out, such as drugs and stealing cars, are social ills affecting many communities and cities throughout England. The Anti-Social Behaviour Orders (ASBO) has allowed authorities powers to deal with such individuals. This will bring them into contact with particular authorities, such as the police, for all the wrong reasons. This first contact between authority, the police and the young person is negative. We see the foundations of mistrust. This has been the focus of so many reports that have examined the causes of riots, but when those involved are from a minority ethnic group this can create further difficulties. Bradford is typical of other inner city areas and although the many regeneration packages have helped to redevelop the city some generic problems remain. These social problems require the communities to work together. The activities of these young people can have a rippling affect on the whole community. The possible increase in the crime rate, and the fear in the community, is much harder to measure.

The boys want to be 'known on the street' and are all part of the 'street cred'. Some argue that citywide curfew orders should be introduced which prevent young people from hanging around after a particular time. This should lead to fewer young people on the streets in the evenings, but others would find their way round this. Crime can have an effect on people in different ways; it can have an emotional as well as a financial effect. Getting one's car stolen causes untold misery but there are other drawbacks. Once an area is labelled as a 'high crime area' it can lead to higher car or household insurance and all the disadvantages of having the wrong postcode. The effect on the whole community is striking,

> 'It don't matter if they're Black or White. Like when they nick someone's car for the parts to sell them off they don't look at whether it belongs to an apna or a White guy obviously it affects everyone' (boy, age 19)

A number of respondents made reference that certain postcodes can become the 'undesirable areas'; these are the 'ones to avoid', if at all possible, because of their high crime rates. Some areas are seen as worse than others. These areas were avoided for other things too, such as their primary and secondary schools. The target of such crime is anyone who has something worthwhile to steal or to commit a crime against. It also denotes a change in time and circumstance from the 'good old days' where one left one's door unlocked. For the older generation this is particularly difficult to come to terms with. The young growing up now can relate to crime and its outcomes much more easily. They know about drugs and crime and what goes in their neighbourhood. They become the eyes and ears for their parents and inform them as to what is going on and they are the community citizens.

One reason for joining gangs, or appearing to break away from the 'family' and the biraderi, may be due to the enormous pressure faced by boys to do well at school and to be successful. The lack of jobs is, of course, an important factor for disengagement. This may be a psychological explanation for the riots in Bradford, but also a cause of exclusion within their own community,

'Get involved in crime and don't want to do anything good, but nothing is simple as that, some lads get up to no good because of the pressure from their parents and relatives, like if they can't fulfil their parent's expectations like get good qualifications, a good job so they totally go away from their parents' (boy, age 19)

In part both the Pakistani male and female sub-culture/gang challenge the authority of their community, but there are also other pressures faced by young people in the wider society . External pressures can almost become an excuse for what is termed as 'mitigating circumstances'. This almost becomes the justification for committing crime and the reason for not going 'straight'. Conflict and confrontation between the two becomes inevitable. In a tight-knit community a gang provides an escape from the everyday restrictions experienced by these young people.

This does not take into account the fear of most ordinary people to report any such activities in case of reprisals. In some cases the community leaders named the young men involved in the disturbances (Allen, 2003) but the vast majority remained quiet in the aftermath of the 1995 disturbances. The confidential reporting of crime to the police has, to an extent, alleviated some of the fears of 'coming forward'. Closer partnerships between individuals, the community and the police are an essential prerequisite in promoting and working towards safer communities.

The activities of the young people, and the fear of being labelled as a base-thi (dishonourable) family, lead to the denial that their sons could not possibly be involved. The importance of maintaining the public image, i.e. chang-ie (good family), is great even when the actions of their sons are illegal. For some this is, perhaps, natural. A family protects their 'good name' but the young people point out the effect it has on the community. Some matters are carefully hidden by those communities involved, since it is in their interest to do so. These matters tend to be ignored by outsiders and any attempt to uncover the truth would bring accusations of racism. The 'naming and shaming' of criminals can be a valuable tool against those who commit crime within the Pakistani community but the very edifice of control itself tends to protect (and therefore promote) gangs. The family and the biraderi can be the focus of adverse publicity and the sense of regret, especially among the older members of the community, is clear.

In the early years of migration and settlement the Pakistani community was largely successful in self-policing itself through the concept of izzat (honour) and the dominant role of the biraderi elders. This is an important reason why most Pakistanis in the early years of settlement as a whole steered clear of public criminal behaviour. This has changed and the biraderi elders are no longer accorded the same respect they once had, especially among sections of their young people. One of the reasons for the development of such violent assertive sub-cultures appears to be the rejection of the norms of an 'alien' society. It is considered a mark of personal, cultural and even of minority ethnic identity, but it appears that another explanation can be the assertive rejection of the norms of the minority ethnic culture. This is not how the parents of any community would wish their children to behave.

Gender as a Sub-culture

The female sub-culture is largely hidden from parents and the biraderi and is normally played out at school or when playing truant from school. It allows girls to get together and offer each other support, often emotional. In this way, gender is a sub-culture. The experience of most girls is quite different from that of their male counterparts. The girls formed small clusters or groups of 'like-minded girls', seemingly going unnoticed. The numbers could be as small as three girls or as many as fifty or more girls. Like all groups of friends they carefully 'vet' who can join them. An existing member usually introduces prospective members.

They would engage in general topics of conversation such as issues of 'freedom', including the right to choose a dress code, or being allowed to wear make-up. They felt restricted in their choice of hairstyle; restricted in their listening to English music and watching English films at home; forbidden to participate in sports after school and at the weekends and forbidden to socialize with friends outside school, even to go to town or to the cinema. Leisure can mean different things to different people: for these girls it means simply going to the city centre for shopping. Freedom was something that could be experienced only outside the confines of the home but the gender divide was clear,

> '...boys have more freedom than girls definitely' (girl, age 16)

Most young people believe that 'Pakistani boys have more freedom than Pakistani girls': seventy-five per cent as opposed to twenty-five per cent who said they do not. Girls were more likely than boys to agree with this (eighty-two per cent v sixty-eight per cent respectively) but it is a fact generally recognized, given that the comment refers to what young people actually get away with rather than what they are supposed to. The appropriate dress code for girls was often an area of tension between parents and girls. Girls were restricted in what they 'can and can't' wear: the parents' preference for them to wear shalwar and kameez over what are considered as Western clothes. The individual choice was often overridden by what is considered as appropriate by the parents. By contrast, no such restriction was placed on their brothers or male cousins, as opposed to the boys who can choose for themselves; it was a point not only made by girls but also boys as well,

> 'Boys mostly do what they want' (boy, age 17)

Girls from many cultures adapt their dress style to when they are out of the family home and some dress as they see fit according to where they go; most, however, get ready at home – they do not need to hide what they do. Pakistani girls considered this as being unfair, even though it meant that challenging the authority of parents was something they would prefer not to do face to face. They would try to avoid direct confrontation. Girls were clear that they had no desire to dress 'sexily' or what some Pakistani parents would regard as 'inappropriately'. It was also clear that most girls wanted to fit in with the other girls in terms of dress.

Some girls were allowed an enormous amount of freedom, for example career choices and to go out with friends, but for others much is hidden from parents. The bedroom, often seen as a place of sanctuary for most young people, was not free from parental surveillance but came under close inspection. The bedroom did not provide a space free from parental control and girls mentioned that parents often searched their bedrooms for Western magazines. In a culture where girls depended on each other they had a certain autonomy and freedom amongst themselves. They were seen as having protection both from men and general outside interference. Modern social life is very different and the threats to the rights of the girls are from their own kind as well as from outside. This indicates that there are more major issues. The result is greater hiding of the separation of tastes, and the need for far more hypocrisy. The common themes on the issue of freedom for boys and girls were pointed out,

'Boys can do what they like, go out with mates, stay out, go out with girls nobody says much, parents and older guys. That's double standards!' (boy, age 19)

Another echoed the same predicament,

'They can wear what they like my brother R got his ear pierced and has long hair my dad don't say nothing to him just me and my younger sister. He can do what he wants I know he's got a White girlfriend' (girl, age 15)

Boys and girls can experience more freedom outside the home, usually at school or at college,

'At school I think most definitely boys and girls have the same amount of freedom…'cos it's the only place where they can' (boy, age 18)

Many girls said that they are prevented from socializing with school friends outside of school hours and were prevented from going outside of the family home unescorted unless they were visiting a relative. The girls were usually chaperoned by their father, mother, aunt or elder married sister. Parents nearly always kept on eye on their siblings' friends, i.e. where they live, the names of their parents, what 'kind' of family they are; in fact most things. Social restrictions are important but are also about being ignored and again the phrase 'double-standards' appears, as the following example points out,

'As for girls they're just ignored with the Pakistanis, they're really restricted, can't socialize after school, meet their friends boys are not that limited…you know how apna are like double-standards' (boy, age 19)

The taste for freedom is common among all young people and the difference is that it is even more hidden. There are other differences, for example, between a Pakistani-born female and a daughter-in-law who is from Pakistan, even though they may be of a similar age. The father and the mother play a dominant role in their lives and uphold decisions made by the heads of the family, but girls do not simply give in to the demands of their parents without a fight,

'Girls are changing and are not easily giving in to the demands of parents' (boy, age 18)

Some stereotypes about the community appear to be true where the father is often seen as being stricter than the mother. As in Pakistan the father is seen as the head of the family and one who makes all the decisions; this is true of some families but not all, but does not mean the mother is a just passive figure. In other families the mother is seen as just as strict as the father and can keep a close eye on what is going since they would primarily be the homemakers. They will make sure rules are followed where the children are concerned and, for example, that the housework is shared out, the children attend the mosque or read the Quran and arrange visits to the homes of the biraderi.

This is similar to Pakistan where older women are the link between the home and the wider biraderi and through visiting they can keep in touch with relatives and share and exchange information. They can access the inner circle of the biraderi where the men cannot. They have a complicated web of friends and relationships and can cut across caste and sect lines, learn about sensitive information such as who will marry whom, and those young people who may be involved in secret relationships,

'My father doesn't want us to go out at night with friends. He doesn't want us to have freedom. But boys can go out anywhere they want, many of them have cars, they hang about in gangs with White girls nobody says anything to them simply because they're boys' (girl, age 16)

On the surface this has parallels with the White community where young girls may be under similar levels of control. Many White parents often agree a suitable time for their sons and daughters to come home on a Saturday night. For many girls the problem is that the majority are forbidden to go outside the home unaccompanied. Boys can do what they like at home and outside are often given a free reign. This is illustrated by the fact that not one single boy mentioned that they felt their parents, or other family members, control them in terms of social restrictions and career aspirations, certainly not to the same extent as girls. Boys were free to socialize after school, eat out, go to the cinema and select their own dress code. Another explained that in her experience many young Pakistani men can be seen in cars driving around during the evenings with their friends and little, if any, restriction is placed on them in terms of what 'they can and can't do' by parents and elders. Boys often sympathized with their sisters' situation.

Summary

Some argue that young people of Pakistani origin live in two separate worlds, the home and the outside. This suggests that young people switch on and off between the two situations, but it is far more complex. There are things that some young people cannot do at home such as dress as they please or wear make-up, but when they arrive home from school they do not simply leave attitudes and thoughts outside the home. They do not switch off their likes and preferences when they are at home and like all young people they continue to think about them.

The riots in Bradford during the summer of 1995 and 2001, and in other cities such as Burnley and Oldham, were to a large extent the result of Pakistani gang-related activities that deliberately instigated the disturbances. One reason for the formation of youth sub-cultures is the result of the tensions that exist within their own community. Boys and girls explained the pressure placed on boys to fulfil their obligations and expectations by obtaining a good education and job. Young people feel the lack of real dialogue with their parents. Although the numbers are relatively small there is an increasing number of young males turning away from their parents and the biraderi to join gangs, which act as a 'substitute family'. The gang provides both emotional and financial security.

Some Pakistani parents are aware of the activities of their sons and can turn a blind eye to criminal behaviour. The fear on the part of parents is clear in terms of the sanctions that are imposed on the base-thi pan-dah (immoral family) by the biraderi. They would prefer certain things to be hidden rather than confront them, and expose them to the awareness of the community. The Pakistani community (and elders) are still in a good position to police its members and these need to be further developed into the broader issue of community policing.

Chapter 12

Islam and the Influence of Culture

Islam remains the bedrock of Pakistani community life in the UK. The ever-increasing numbers of mosques that have been built, or recently opened, are an indication of the importance of Islam and congregations are large in number. Religion is the perceived mark of identity and distinction and is also a way of justifying attitudes; it is of palpable cultural significance to them. This is well illustrated by the evidence presented here, where the vast majority of young people sampled believe that Islam remains a significant part of their lives (and of their parents' lives too). The parents welcome this as it denotes the continuation of Islam onto the next generation of young people. Most referred to Islam as a way of life and a complete way of living if the tenets of Islam are followed.

Islam, and what is written in the Quran, is clearly marked out. The real difficulty lies in examining the cultural attitudes of the community. The cultural attitudes play a significant role and have, to a greater extent, even taken over religious ones; it is the usual religious definitions that underlie the social and research approaches to the Pakistani community. Young people's rejection was of cultural attitudes and values rather than religion itself. Indeed, they made a point of noticing the conflict between the two. The Pakistanis are no different to most other communities.

The argument that the young have lost some of their commitment to religion appears to be unfounded at this particular moment in time. In terms of attendance at mosque, 52 per cent of young people said they go to the mosque. This is much higher compared to those who attend church, and in the breakdown of the data nine per cent of young people said they attend the mosques 'rarely', 21 per cent attend 'sometimes' and 22 per cent attend 'regularly'. This may appear low but the reason for this was that these young people attended the mosque at different ages. Some would start as early as four years of age and complete the Quran by seven or eight, while others would start at eight and finish when they are eleven or twelve years of age.

Not all young people attended the mosque. Some went to a relative's house or someone who is part of the biraderi's house to learn the Quran. Others are taught the Quran at home by parents. Teaching normally takes place in small groups and parents can monitor their child's progress, but perhaps more importantly the family or friends know the person who is in charge is trustworthy. Whether they are taught in a mosque or elsewhere, collective learning was something to be revered and held sacred. Learning in this environment also provided emotional support: as mothers dropped their children at class they often stayed and had a cup of tea with other mothers. This was important as it allowed mothers to meet and chat about everyday issues.

Most young people happily attended the mosque because it was something that all young people 'did'. The obligation to read the Quran, the Kalama and the Namaz was something that was instilled into these young people at an early age. They grow up seeing male adults attend the mosque for Namaz or when they go to read Eid (Namaz). Most fathers take their son(s) to the mosque from an early age to read the Namaz in order to familiarize them with the surroundings. This also created a sense of community. Attending mosque was like attending school; it was expected of them; it is something that they must do, but there were some instances highlighted where some boys (and girls) were pushed by parents or relatives to go to the mosque.

Major gender differences were found in other areas: boys were much more likely than girls to attend the mosque (91 per cent v 16 per cent). Boys were also more likely than girls to go to the mosque 'regularly' (thirty-nine per cent v six per cent). Whereas fathers would take their sons to the mosque only a small number of girls said they could attend the mosque to read the Namaz or were allowed to attend the special Eid prayers, but given the opportunity some would like to attend. However, for most women the alternative was to pray at home either alone or in the company of other women such as family or relatives. Bradford is unusual in some instances as in other cities such as London females are welcomed by Imams and are allowed to pray in the mosque but are separated from the men, and this allows as many people as possible to attend the mosque.

All young people considered Islam as being 'important' to them and an equal numbers of boys and girls expressed this (100 per cent v 100 per cent respectively), but just over a quarter considered themselves to be 'religious' (26 per cent). Gender differences were found: boys were more likely than girls to consider themselves as 'religious' (34 per cent v 18 per cent respectively). This is different from some research that shows Muslim women are more 'religious' than Muslim men. The vast majority considered Islam to be 'important'; although some did not believe themselves to be 'religious',

'No, I'm not (religious). I go to the mosque…but Islam is very important' (boy, age 15)

Most young people had an idea of who is considered to be religious; it meant reading the Namaz five times a day, keeping all the Ramzans (fasting) and reading the Quran regularly. Good actions and deeds were at the centre of being considered by others to be 'religious'. After the initial completion some only attended the mosque on special occasions, for example on Jumma (Friday prayers) and on Eid, while others attended regularly, as the results of this study demonstrate. A point was made by a small number of young people that relatives (or friends) are 'pushed' while others are forced by parents to attend the mosque,

'Some of my cousins are forced to go to the mosque when they don't want to' (girl, age 16)

Other young people also observed this,

'Some friends I know their parents force them to go the mosque. I don't think there's any point to that since your heart's not in it…one of my friends Z was forced by his dad to fast, so he used to get up in the morning begin the fast and then go to school and have his school dinner there, I felt sorry for him' (boy, age 18)

Unlike school, playing truant from mosque lessons was practically impossible. Non-attendees would be reprimanded and the parents would be informed immediately. It was interesting to note that no respondent in the sample admitted that they ever had played truant from the mosque. For some, especially the younger ones, being forced to attend mosque or to keep Ramzan (fast) is common. Some young people did not want to attend the house because they were bullied either on the way or while in the mosque. This situation was made worse especially if the bully/bullies also attended the same school as the young person. Parents were often oblivious to what was happening.

Attending the mosque regularly was a sign of commitment both to Islam and to the community. Public observance is crucial because it is directly linked to one's status in the family and the biraderi. Others judge the individual in terms of his/her religiousness as opposed to being allowed to have a personal and private relationship with Islam. Those who attend the mosque are given a given a higher social standing, whilst those who do not are labelled as being wayward. Attendance demonstrates to the biraderi that their son is being taught the 'say-ee' (right) way with the 'say-ee' (right) morals, which include obedience and loyalty. This suggests that some young people attend the mosque not out of choice but to increase their standing among biraderi members. This is all very public and can be compared to the Victorian age where church attendance was almost like being compulsory.

Several young people highlighted that the language of instruction used by most Imams and mosque teachers was Urdu and/or Azad Kashmiri Punjabi. For those who were genuinely bilingual in these languages they could understand instructions given by those in charge of the class, but for others who had limited skills in their 'native' language this proved to be a difficult period of learning. They often fell behind in their learning and took much longer to learn the Quran. The ones who had difficulty in understanding tended to rely on friends to interpret for them in terms of what the Imam was saying and this appears to be overlooked by most parents. There are a few mosques in Bradford that are actively trying to overcome this problem and the language of instruction is English. It is interesting to note how Arabic is taught to young people through instructions in Urdu, Azad Kashmiri Punjabi, English or indeed through a combination of languages.

Some point out that the role of the mosque should not only be to teach the Quran but also things such as offering counselling or career advice to young people. In another way the Imams should be role models for young people to look up to, much as parents and teachers. Imams have an important role to play both in the community and outside. For example they could be the bridge between schools and parents, and schools could relay information through the Imams intended for parents and closer links could be formed to promote schooling. Imams are influential members of their communities and this could be used in a positive way. Most young people acknowledged the importance of Islam to older Pakistanis such as their parents, uncles and aunts, at least on the surface,

> 'People like old people, are always going on about how we should live according to Islam but it's not like that, people like gora (White people) think we do, like have long beards, cover our legs. It's the image' (girl, age 16)

Elders are also seen to use Islam in order to control young people, as the following girl points out. Listening to parents and elders is essential for passing on kinds of traditions and values, but some young people see it quite differently,

> 'Parents just use it when they want to, like they say kids should listen to elders, it's in Islam' (girl, age 16)

For this young girl the contradictions in the attitudes of many parents and the clash between religious and cultural values are clear,

> 'Well, like I said in Islam they should have [the] same freedoms and also like in marriage, people should have the choice, you can't force young people especially girls to get a forced marriage' (girl, age 16)

In theory the distinction between the two is clear but in practice the two have in many ways become fused. Another young person talked about the 'fusion' of Islam and culture and the contradictions that arise out of this,

> 'It's all culture and Islam mixed together...most of the parents follow culture, like girls leave school' (girl, age 19)

But she realizes that things could well be different;

> 'If they properly followed Islam, things would be different' (ibid)

Central to the argument of most young people is understanding on the part of parents and elders of whichever religious persuasion. The importance of Islam to parents is clear and the majority of the sample said they would say their parents are 'religious' (young people were free to interpret what 'religious' means). The importance of caste and religious sect remains for the majority of Pakistani parents, which the young clearly reject but the old still hold on to.

Parents and Islam

The vast majority (99 per cent) said that their parents consider Islam as being 'important'. On the one level the young people accepted the importance of Islam to their parents but at the same time they recognize that the actual behaviour of parents can be cultural and, on occasions, contradictory to the rules of Islam. Yet despite this, they point out that in terms of religiousness, the majority of young people said their parents are 'religious' (94 per cent). The young wanted their parents and elders to be religious. The importance of the Hajj remains an important part of the lives of Pakistanis. The Hajj is symbolic and verifies belonging to a unique and exclusive club in that only a select few are blessed with going on it in their life. Sometimes financial pressures do not permit the individual to go on Hajj, while on other occasions ill health may be a deciding factor. Going on Hajj was still something expected of all individuals, especially those who live in the UK,

'My father will be going on Hajj next year. They are like all of my family and relatives' (boy, age 19)

Others have been on Hajj more than once. The reason for this can be because this girl's grandparents may have died; the Hajj must be performed in their name first. It is performed 'in place' of the deceased,

'My dad's really religious, he's been on Hajj three times now' (girl, age 17)

Every year two million people from all over the world congregate for Hajj for a once in a lifetime experience. People from all castes, sects and creeds pray together where everyone is considered to be equal; no one is above or higher than the next person. This is how most of the young people in the sample understand Islam: a sense of pureness. In terms of mosque attendance of the fathers 16 per cent of young people said their father visits the mosque 'rarely'; 33 per cent attend 'sometimes' and just under half (46 per cent) attend 'regularly',

'My father never misses his Namaz if he misses one of them he'll read extra in the evening also my mother she never misses if she can help it' (boy, age 14)

In rural parts of Pakistan such as Mirpur time is allocated to read Namaz, especially the Jumma (Friday) prayers. Although most women in the rural parts of Pakistan do not have the opportunity to attend the mosque it does not mean they miss out. Most either read at home or in small congregations in the company of women in a mutually agreed location. This also gives women time to catch up on gossip and general chit-chat about what is happing in the community. Equally importantly they get to learn about any jobs that may be available for their husbands or sons. It is a time to cement existing ties and make new friends. Despite the change in terms of geographical location, praying Namaz five times a day has continued among the older Pakistanis. Those young people who are devoted find the time to read the Namaz either during work time, i.e. during lunch and break times, given the flexibility allowed by their employer, or they can read extra rak-kahs in the evening Namaz.

Sects, castes and the Pakistani 'community'

The complexity of the 'Pakistani community' is well illustrated through examining the tradition of sect and caste. The biraderi have their own traditions and values. The biraderi can include a religious sect and/or caste. Like all the major religions of the world there are many smaller religious sects. Islam appears to be similar in this respect to other world religions. The two main sects are Sunni and Shia but other smaller sects exist, for example, Whah-bbism. This also applies to the many caste groups. The major castes are Raja and Jat, often referred to by Pakistanis as jaz-zati (landed); Bengse (smaller holdings), followed by lower castes such as Morchi (shoesmith) and Majaar (landless, travellers). There are many caste groups who perform various jobs according to their standing in the community. The biraderis should not be treated as homogeneous group and their traditions can be just as different as those between caste groups.

The young people were open and frank about their experiences and were willing to explain some of the problems these divisions have created in their community. The majority said their community is not homogeneous and strong religious and cultural divisions exist based on age, gender, caste and religious sect. From an early age individuals become aware of the major divisions that exist within their community (sometimes as opposed to the more general societal divisions),

> 'There are others like you know, based on the korm-ma (caste)…but caste is important on the surface parents don't say much but they always prefer to people as Jats, Bhen-gse, that they are bad, arrogant' (boy, age 19)

This labelling of individuals and groups is common: where differences are marked out this is like being in a different class from one's neighbour or friend. Each caste likes to think of itself as being somehow different or 'higher' than the next one. It has also created problems for integration and community cohesion but this is overlooked. What the young people see as striking are those divisions that exist between different communities and the effect this can have on mixing with individuals from other communities. On a different level the community in question is no different from other 'Asian' or from the White/English majority communities, which in some cases place barriers between themselves and others,

> '…also between apna and White people and the Indians' (boy, age 19)

This suggests how communities can have internal divisions and on another level have external ones too, such as those between different communities. Some of this is due to misunderstanding and much of it is based on prejudice, whether racial or religious. What is surprising for some is the lack of dialogue between communities and this highlights the dangers of segregation; not a geographical one but one based on minds. The young talk not only about the external divisions but also the internal ones that are more immediate. The root cause of these divisions is 'cultural' but it also reveals the deeper differences based on religion,

'Cultural! As you know in Islam, everybody is equal, with no one higher than the other. But we, between Sunnis, Shias, Whah-bbies we shouldn't have groups and just follow Islam and nothing else' (boy, age 19)

These young people portray a generic meaning of Islam where all Muslims are seen as equal and there are no divisions between Muslims: all Muslims are considered as 'brothers' and 'sisters'. The young people were quick to point out that the Mulvis (religious leaders) are to blame,

'A lot of my friends and I blame the old people especially these Mulvis. I think they're the ones who created this mess' (boy, age 19)

The young were clear that these divisions often affect their everyday life. For example it is rare for Muslims to attend a mosque that is of a different religious sect to one's own beliefs and, as in Pakistan, this holds true in Britain also,

'...like you have korms (caste groups) and sects like Sunnis, Shias and Whah-bbies, they never get on or go to each other's mosques even on Eid' (boy, age 19)

For these young people cultural traditions are un-Islamic, are wrong and no longer applicable. This suggests that many young people are rejecting traditional attitudes, arguing that beneath the surface 'we're are all Muslims' regardless of religious sects or caste and this is a way of declaring independence from sectarian control,

'They put everyone into separate groups even though we're all Muslims. I think that's definitely wrong' (girl, age 16)

This shows the complexity of the Pakistani 'community' and the broader argument that there is no one community but many communities exist within the broad heading of the 'Pakistani community'. The public discussion of an individual's caste is common and is part of everyday life. The caste of an individual is discussed in public by parents and relatives and the awareness is that parents are attempting to maintain superficial barriers between groups even though it is against Islam,

'As I said we own a shop on W. A. Road and we get a lot of customers. My father and mother always say they're Mor-chi, Bhen-gse, Jats, they refer to everyone by caste, so I think caste is important to them. Also when someone comes into the shop during the day my parents and aunts say they are Shias or they are Whah-bbi' (girl, age 16)

Where parents continue to place importance on religious sect and caste and make distinctions, the young people's attitudes are strikingly different. They reveal a modern and cosmopolitan attitude,

'I don't ask my friends what caste they are I don't care as long as they're good to me and we have a laugh. I remember my father and relatives going on about that you shouldn't talk to kids who are Shia that they're not nice people, they still say that now. Like I said it's wrong' (girl, age 17)

The effect of these attitudes and how they trickle down into everyday community life was pointed out by most. This often means limited integration at social events between members of different religious sects and caste origin,

'You know when you go to a wedding you only see your own biraderi (kin members) and no one outside of that' (boy, age 18)

This reveals the 'exclusion within exclusion' that exists within the Pakistani community. This can be seen in Bradford and also throughout the United Kingdom in traditional immigrant cities such as Birmingham and Leicester. The G. H. district of Bradford is home to many mosques, which have been built and run by different sects. Members donate money to help build the mosque and help with renovation costs, and money is collected during Jumma (Friday prayers) and also by door-to-door collections. All of this suggests that the close links with cultural heritage continue to play a significant part among older Pakistanis; but at the same time young people are refusing to take on board those values linked more to rivalry between groups than distinction of religion.

Affluent families who belong to caste groups such as Rajahs, or Jats have raised sufficient funds from individuals or families within their own caste to built the mosque without having to rely on those outside the family, especially individuals who may be of a lower caste and who also can be base-thi (shameful). Suggesting superiority of one group over another in giving money to help raise funds to build a mosque is a public act, as opposed to giving in secret, which is more religious. Families have contributed funds made through family businesses, for example restaurants, shops and property on rent. The name(s) of the family(s) involved who helped financially in building the mosque is held in high regard among the biraderi both in Bradford and also in Pakistan. In communal events such as weddings and religious gatherings, the name of the korm (caste) and the family is respected. The building of a new mosque has religious significance and publicly demonstrates the wealth of the family or the korm.

The point is that much of this is very public when compared with the Western style of giving to charity, where money for good causes is often given in secret. Money given to charity by a high caste family publicly is viewed by the biraderi as a status of their wealth. The point is that contributing financially to building a mosque is not an indication of being religious but an indication of social standing. All this points to how cultural practices are legitimized through religion and the far greater complexity of the beliefs and values of the Pakistani community. It is extremely rare for an individual to attend a mosque that belongs to another sect. Many might like to attend the mosque close to their house but are forbidden by family members to attend a mosque that belongs to a different religious sect. Given the choice many would go to the nearest mosque regardless of sect or caste affiliation. Despite this the pressure of the clan on the extended family is strong,

'We go to the mosque on... it's a Shia mosque all our relatives go there and I have to go there' (boy, age 18)

Another explained,

> '…my father prefers to go there my father says that Sunnis go to … so we go to the one on ….' (boy, age 14)

In the case of this example he is forbidden to attend a mosque which has a different sect affiliation to his own. This is a common experience for most young people and socializing with other sect members also appears to be restricted,

> 'It doesn't just apply to going to the mosque but all the other things like people won't go to homes of Whah-bbies or Sunnis' (boy, age 18)

This represents the formation of separate groups. The young people argued all of this is against the Law of Islam and if they had the choice they would attend the mosque nearest to their house, regardless of sect affiliation but they saw these were the expectations. The change in attitude is clear among young people,

> 'I think it's all silly' (boy, age 18)

This has parallels with other religions, for example, Christianity also has sub-divisions: Catholics and Protestant churches or, for example, Jehovah's Witnesses and Mormon churches have their own religious beliefs. The second point to remember is that a superficial divide between various groups creates smaller communities, in the case of the community in question, biraderis based on religious sect and caste who have their own distinct traditions, values and norms. The young people gave personal accounts where such divisions affect their everyday lives. The young argue that these serve to divide rather than unite Pakistani Muslims and these divisions are as strong as those that exist between different communities, i.e. between Pakistanis and Indians and those between the majority Whites and the 'Asians'.

Marriage

It should be clear by now that the Pakistani community is much more than just about (forced) arranged marriages, something which is often highlighted but it is synonymous with the Pakistanis. This often grabs the headlines: girls running away to escape a marriage that has been planned by parents and the biraderi. Few however make the distinction between marriage, an arranged marriage and a forced arranged marriage. We do not need to have a precise definition of what these are the young people interviewed themselves suitably provided the definitions for our purposes. All young people in the sample said they would like to get married, settle down and have children. They did not reject marriage or what it stands for but they wanted a say in who their partner would be. Marriage was seen as something for life and sacred and not to enter into lightly. Marriage was seen as the bedrock of their community. Their prospective partner was seen as someone for life and divorce continues to be frowned upon not only by the biraderi but also by the young people themselves.

The issue of marriage would also demonstrate the differences in expectation of boys and girls. This was not because parents intentionally treated boys and girls differently but because the traditional norms continue to play an important role. Among the many issues discussed arranged marriage was the one that struck home for most. They could relate to and understand it from other people's experience. Many older girls in the sample knew that marriage was something planned for them in the not too distant future. The boys knew that they could get away from an arranged marriage for at least several years more, but both knew that marriage would be inevitable. In their everyday experience they knew that some marriages worked well and others worked less well and it was these that had an enormous influence on them.

'Choice' was a fundamental issue on which young people were not willing to back down. This would prove to cause enormous tension both within the household and also within the biraderi. This would cut across sect, caste and biraderi lines. They were explicit about the right of the individual to choose. They did not reject marriage or family life but saw it as something positive that they would like to experience. They disagreed on how it was instigated and how young people were exposed to it. The rights granted under Islam were pointed out by most,

'In Islam every person has the final choice who to marry as long as they are Muslim or they convert to Islam' (boy, age 19)

Most young people were clearly against the idea of entering into a forced arranged marriage. A forced marriage is one where the parents or elders decided rather than the young people having any say. For the young the important thing was the freedom to choose, and a 'real' choice was something most thought they would not have,

'I don't, not a forced one. I want to decide a marriage partner myself' (boy, age 19)

This posed a challenge to the authority of the parents to decide what is in the best interest of their children. The young would argue that this could be applicable to the young people in Pakistan where the situation is different, but in the British context it is the young people who have a greater experience and exposure to British life than their parents. This does not mean that the young would simply impose a marriage partner on their parents. Young people wanted their parents and elders to be part of the selection process. They wanted to introduce a prospective partner to their parents, followed by ceremonial exchange of visits, a period of getting to know one another and also getting to know the partner's family and relatives. This would take several months rather than weeks to complete and they insisted that their parents' opinion would be taken on board in the whole process; while others would happily rely on their parents to find a suitable marriage partner.

Marriage was seen as a start to a process of events and all the expectations that go with being married. Marriage is not just seen as a union between two people but a union between families. Once married the pressure to start a family would be considerable. The young people sampled were aware that if they got married to someone of their parents' choosing then they will receive various benefits such as free board and other economic support, in fact most things that parents are able to help with. Providing a deposit for a house and a car is not untypical.

The majority of young people (78 per cent) believe that 'forced arranged marriages are a bad thing' (where the partner is simply chosen by others) as opposed to 12 per cent who believe that 'arranged marriages are a good thing' (one that allows an individual the right to select or refuse a partner). The remaining ten per cent said they were 'unsure'. What was striking was that not a single young person who said they were intending to enter marriage was doing so out of choice, but at the request of parents. Most boys acknowledged the enormous pressure placed on girls to get married. Girls were more likely than boys to consider arranged marriages to be a 'bad thing' (81 per cent v 74 per cent). This reveals a generational change from the traditional attitudes of many parents, i.e. the preference for arranged marriage, as opposed to allowing young people the freedom to choose. They referred to the experience of others and learnt some of the more negative aspects, that a marriage may not be a happy one. They often start from this,

'I've seen a lot of people who have had an arranged marriage; they're not happy at all' (boy, age 19)

This did not mean that they remained quiet. Traditional habits were continually being questioned and eroded by the young generation. The important issue is a change of attitudes over time. For many of them it is too late, but at the same time they accept that only they can change attitudes of parents (and the community), whether through communication or conflict, or at least differ in attitudes towards their own children. Being pushed into marriage brought out all the negative ideas rather than it being the 'happiest day of your life'. Only the preferred relatives and friends would be invited as opposed to all the biraderi. Parents and elders take charge of the important day and decide the itinerary, such as the mania and the mehndi (the ritual wedding preparations). Pakistani marriages tend to be based on renewing old and forming new relationships. This did not necessarily make them 'bad' parents but they were considered to be living in the past. For these parents clearly the point of reference was the village and this was seen as something old and in the past. Most Pakistani parents acknowledge that their sons could be involved in relationships with girls, particularly goria (White) girls and sometimes they actively looked out for clues,

'Go out with girls, nobody says much parents and older guys' (boy, age 19)

This rule generally applies only when the boy is seeing a White girl, but the reaction is quite different if the Pakistani boy is having a relationship with a Pakistani girl. This is frowned upon by the biraderi as being base-thi (shameful, immoral behaviour) especially out of caste or sect relationships. If the boy is in a relationship with a White girl there are often no serious implications from the girl's family/relatives since she is non-Pakistani and promiscuity is accepted. Labels and stereotypes play an important role. The types of punishment are clear,

> '...it'll be embarrassing and shameful, base-thi (shameful), especially if relatives found out as you know if I was a girl it would be Pakistan for some serious rehabilitation! A quick marriage that would be the prescription' (boy, age 19)

There is a tendency to think of the few examples of forced arranged marriage and consider this as a normal practice of the community. Like all, they wish to have a choice, a real choice of their future partner. Where this was available the young people welcomed parental or biraderial involvement in their marriage plans. It was a time of joy and celebration over a period of several weeks – even longer in Pakistan – and it is a time for all the biraderi to enjoy. Culturally, girls are viewed as upholding the izzat of the family and any deviance from this has to be severely punished for tarnishing the honour of the immediate family and the biraderi, but the girls do not see it this way. The severe consequences are clear for engaging in a relationship with the opposite sex and 'one that hits home',

> 'I know definitely one of the girls got beaten up by her father he just took her out of school. I haven't seen her since' (girl, age 16)

Freedom of choice is preferred over the wishes of parents. In fact 83 per cent of young people believe that 'a boy and girl should be allowed to select a partner themselves' and only eight per cent said a boy and a girl should 'rely on their parents'. Both boys and girls equally said they would prefer to 'select their own (marriage) partner' (83 per cent v 82 per cent respectively) and only a small number of young people said they should 'rely on their parents' to find them a suitable marriage partner (eight per cent and eight per cent respectively).

The majority is in favour of selecting a marriage partner of their choice rather than rely on their parents. They believe they are capable of finding a partner themselves. It is interesting to note that many young people were in a relationship at the time of their interviews. It is as if parents do not think their young are capable of finding someone suitable. The parents' fear is both clear and obvious to them, even though misplaced; if young people are allowed the freedom then they may choose someone who is from a different caste or religious sect. The belief that arranged marriage is a ''bad thing' was widespread. It is a practice that they argue is outdated and relevant only in Pakistan,

> 'bad, bad thing. They were good for old people that was in Pakistan that was then, times have changed, it's just that a lot of Pakistanis haven't accepted this' (girl, age 19)

On the question of freedom to choose the answer was explicit and clear,

> '...young people should have the final say' (girl, age 19)

Another issue raised is the 'incompatibility' of spouses from Pakistan,

'...which has caused tension, arguments and fights between the girl who is from here and the husband from Pakistan' (girl, age 16)

Some young people in the sample wanted to get married in Pakistan while most said they would prefer their partner to be British (born and raised in the UK). Most boys ands girls in the sample wanted their partner to have some formal qualifications or at least be able to converse in the English language. Higher academic attainment (such as a degree or professional qualifications) was always looked upon favourably, especially by parents. Like all individuals, they wanted a partner that they could relate to and build a caring relationship with. There has been much debate about the suitability of spouses from abroad. Differences in attitudes, culture and language have meant that the community is often accused of pairing incompatible spouses together. This is often against the will of the parties concerned. There have been a number of high-profile cases where this has been highlighted, but all young people see this as a 'bad thing'. Some actually want to marry someone from Pakistan with whom they may share a similar background in terms of sect and caste.

Parents still hold a sense of responsibility and loyalty to relatives in Pakistan, where they are seen as helping by marrying their children from there. Once the spouse comes to the UK they can provide for their own family through sending remittances. The sense of obligation to relatives remains strong. This is where most young people believe that a break from tradition is not necessarily bad. The underlying motives behind arranged marriages were clear to some young people: the desire among parents to maintain family links with relatives in Pakistan,

'Most parents want their kids to marry their cousins simply because they want them to get into Britain and nothing else' (boy, age 18)

The pressure from parents, in-laws and the biraderi to remain married was also evident. Divorce is publicly frowned upon especially when instigated by the girl, and the base-thi (shame, loss of honour) is clear for parents,

'They take the attitude that if a marriage breaks up then it would be base-thi (shame) for the whole family and not just the two individuals' (girl, age 16)

And, recognizing the denial of the real situation, this girl added,

'In this and other ways parents and relatives deny everything what is really happening within Pakistani families' (ibid)

This has strengths in terms of support and mutual help. On the one hand some of the weaknesses are obvious, for example having to stay married and the lack of freedom to decide and the control exercised by the biraderi. For many Pakistani parents a bride or groom from Pakistan re-enforces traditional values and the authority of the husband and loyalty to the biraderi. The important issue is the extent of control over girls, which is subject to the conditions and the values of the 'community'. The wishes of the biraderi members often override the wishes of the parents. Parents are socialized to believe that a bride or groom will be dutiful and loyal. Despite all the research evidence stereotypes remain: parents argue that eth-tha nay gor-ia luggar (girls from Britain are immoral) and outha nay goria changia (girls from Pakistan are loyal and respectful). These young people also made clear that they are more than capable of finding a partner themselves,

> 'There is enough boys and girls going out with each other and I think they are more than capable of finding someone themselves' (boy, age 18)

It was a constant worry for parents and made more complicated if the boy and the girl who are dating are of a different caste (or sect),

> 'They are constantly worried their son or daughter may be going out with someone who is of a different caste or is not a Sunni' (ibid)

The effect on the young people who are in this situation and their sense of helplessness is clear,

> 'I think a lot of young people are really screwed up they don't make many decisions about their life' (ibid)

In communal discussions and in everyday contact the biraderis encourage parents to get their young children married (especially daughters). It is considered as nake chann-ga kam (the honourable way). For the community marriage between biraderi members ensures the girl does not have the opportunity to bring base-thi (disrespect) on the family, for example by mixing with boys or forming undesirable relationships. Discussion about marriage is periodic and inevitable, an important process towards marriage. At first friendly open persuasion is used by relatives that her prospective husband is a chann-ga pora (he is a good person) and his parents are chann-ga pandah (they are good, respectable people). The important point to remember is that the girl concerned is made to feel special at every stage of the wedding procedure. It is customary for relatives to ask parents sou-nay keth nay ba so (how much gold are you going to give to your daughter). Again this is to encourage the girl to accept an arranged marriage, and with the partner of her parents' choice.

The ras-tha dar (relatives) also transmit the norms of the specific biraderi to individuals. For example often there is talk of 'only when you have a husband you get izzat bhan-ni' (the way to gain respect within the biraderi is to get married). The biraderi also makes clear that koi ney zin-dthi (there is no life without a husband). The influence of the biraderi over parents was also clear to the point that the 'biraderi' decides the important issues like suitable marriage partner and where to settle,

> 'Well everything like where to buy land in Pakistan, what kind of house to build' (boy, age 14)

As well as issues that concerned young people on a more personal level, such influence suggests the sentimental attachment to Pakistan, 'where to get the best riz-tha (prospective marriage partner) for me and my younger brother, so it's everything' (ibid)

Divorce, as in other many cultures, is associated with considerable stigma. It can have a profound effect on individuals and families within the Pakistani community. At one level parents will argue that it will be base-thi if the marriage ends and on another divorce is seen as having a destabilizing effect on the established extended kinship structure. The majority of marriages that take place are between close biraderi members. Divorce can often cause nar-razey (conflict) between individuals and/or families. Although there are few statistics on this issue there are an increasing number of girls who are separated from their partner but are not divorced, at least under English law. This can have repercussions on biraderi life. The importance of marriage can be seen from the thousands of pounds that are spent on airfares, accommodation, food, the cost of the Nikka (marriage ceremony), the Waal-lima (marriage festivities) and obtaining an entry visa for the spouse to settle in the United Kingdom.

Summary

The young people highlight that the attitudes of parents and elders can be of a different cultural view. Cultural (rather than Islamic) values are difficult to explain since both cultural and Islamic values have been fused together through past generations. The belief in Islam remains strong, both among the older and the young population, and this will continue in the future. However some of the cultural practices and influences are likely to be dismissed as outdated.

Chapter 13

Conclusion

The conclusion is a telling one. At a time of suspicion about the Muslim community reflected in a changing global situation, particularly in light of 9/11 and 7/7, it marks a change in how (ethnic) communities are seen by those from outside, the emphasis shifted from 'Pakistanis' to 'Muslim' and great deal of examination.

These young people were like most other teenagers: they were open about their experiences, feelings and attitudes, even sometimes critical. Their opinions do not represent 'official' views of parents or the community. They were quick to point out areas of tension and conflict and challenge their parents and elders. The evidence presented in this book reveals a changing situation in the experience of young people (and older Pakistanis). This is partly a reflection of their increased assimilation (rather than integration) into the wider British society as their tastes and preferences become like their White/English counterparts'. Parents can see this as a threat to their cultural values. This poses a challenge not only for their community but also for the wider indigenous communities. Much of the existing research points to differences between young people of 'Asian' origin and 'White' young people but rarely engages in their similarities. We often think of the differences between ethnic groups but this is equally applied to all young people. What was true of the older generation does not hold true for the next generation of all young people. It should also be clear from this book that young people and parents have a strong loyalty to the United Kingdom and what it stands for.

Ethnic communities are often homogenized, for example Pakistanis, Indians and Bangladeshis are often referred to as 'Asians', which does not take into account the many differences that exist 'between' 'Asians' or indeed the greater diversity 'within' the groups based on caste, sect, culture or language to name but four. This is equally true of the 'White' community, which is also homogenized to the point where differences or diversity are overlooked or at worse ignored. 'White' communities are treated as being the same as each other (like the Asians). This rarely takes into account the differences say between the English, Welsh, Scottish or the Irish which are so symbolically illustrated during sporting events but are overlooked in terms of research. Yet there is also a sense of Britishness at events such as athletics or during the Olympics.

Community segregation took on a new meaning in light of the 2001 disturbances: the focus of so much debate centred on 'Black/Asian' communities, which are on the whole segregated from the 'White' community and this is reflected in housing. This overlooks the fact that some (minority) communities have a cultural preference to live near their relatives irrespective of their ethnic origin. Some individuals may prefer to live in the countryside while others prefer city life. The problem is that community integration fails to take into account the enormous diversity of the UK population.

The population make-up of the UK is enormously diverse, with old minorities such as Pakistanis or Indians with established social and economic links in the UK and new minorities such as asylum seekers and refugees arriving much more recently (and in different circumstances). The emphasis is on the new minorities to adjust to British society quicker or they can become part of a secluded (or alienated) community. This poses a challenge to policy makers and institutions but also to the general population in terms of how they perceive asylum seekers. This poses questions around community segregation. The pretext is that such groups will be segregated from the 'White' population. It is argued they will also be segregated from the old minority communities like the Pakistanis or the Indians. It is also ignored that asylum seekers can be the targets of hostility from all groups irrespective of their ethnic or racial origin (and not just from 'White' people). One important question is how much have these young people absorbed the traditions and values of their parents? Certain traditional attitudes remain significant, for example the importance of Islam; others such as the rules regarding marriage or dress code will continue to be eroded as the young argue their point of view.

Like in most communities the underlying cause of generational tension is the lack of communication and understanding on the part of parents and has led to a breakdown in communication between the generations. Real feelings are often hidden from parents (and elders) where they do not talk to parents about anything of personal importance, for example, bullying. There is a strong sense of alienation among young people. Often overlooked is that young people can be marginalized within their own community, which can inhibit their aspirations. This leads to a lack of decision-making power for young people, who are assumed to follow instructions from parents and the biraderi as if they are 'blank slates'. Young people are clearly told what to do and when they resist generational tensions arise. 'Respect' has religious significance but it is also used to attempt to control the behaviour of young people. While in front of elders young people do show respect; when they are out of sight they display their real feelings. Authority and control is revered by the biraderi but at the same time young people despise overt attempts to control.

Beneath the surface there are many causes of generational tensions: the attitudes of older Pakistanis who believe they are 'Pakistani' in terms of their nationality and identity despite the length of stay and adaptation to circumstances. The sentimental attachment to Pakistan, and to those relatives still left behind, remains strong where regular contact is maintained through visits and marriage. The vast majority of young people in this sample consider they are British and Britain is 'home'. They have a strong preference for English culture such as literature, dress and language. Some argue that 'Asian' young people live in two separate worlds, but their experiences are more like their White/English counterparts.

Certain traditional attitudes remain significant. The biraderi remains a powerful institution that has enormous power over individuals and parents. This suggests that parents submit to the power of the biraderi without challenging or questioning its norms. The benefits of remaining within the biraderi – where nepotism plays an important role, for example through interest-free loans, providing false documents in order to purchase property or to obtain loans – is clear. Nepotism is considered part of everyday life among Pakistanis, but can considered as being corrupt when some families are treated in a more favourable manner than others.

One way of ensuring conformity is through labelling, which plays an important role in making sure that individuals and families remain loyal to the biraderi. This is done on a number of levels. Among its biraderi members parents are encouraged to exercise strict control over their offspring and decisions reflect the attitude and the traditions of the biraderi. In some biraderis the son is encouraged to stay on at school and to go to university and the daughter is encouraged, and in some cases forced, to leave school, stay at home or get married. Control is all too important for the biraderi.

Recent debates about the nature of racism have included institutional racism. We have to be clear about which institutions are under scrutiny. Does it only include statutory institutions? What about voluntary organizations; can they also be the targets of criticism? The problem with the word 'racism' is that it implies that only White people can be racist and only 'White' institutions are in a position to disadvantage Black/Asian people. This is a naive assumption. It does not take into account that White individuals or communities can also feel disadvantaged. Sometimes there is an institutional failure (rather than institutional racism) that is under scrutiny. Institutional racism lays the blame on 'institutions' rather than the individual and overlooks personal prejudice or personal hatred. Racism has a narrow meaning. There are many forms of racism. It should not mean that only Whites can be racist, but that Black/Asian people can also be racist. Until recently this has been overlooked. These are all forms of racism.

There are perhaps two key phrases that emerge from this book and which encapsulate the complexity and the tension of the experiences of the young. The first is the word 'hypocrites'. Many young people point out the levels of hypocrisy, suggesting that the morals of Islam are twisted to suit the interests of personal and family power. The elders are depicted as saying one thing and doing another, or trying to retain control by exploiting notions of 'izzat'. They undermine the social equilibrium of the young by citing their present values and interests as 'kufr'. This undermines the sense of well-being in the young. Which other groups are told they live as 'aliens' in their own environment? It also causes hypocrisy in them. If they are not allowed to behave naturally then they behave in one way for their parents and in another, including a different style of language, for their peers. In this particular community the distinction between the two is extreme. There are two separate codes, of dress as well as taste, of habit as well as behaviour. So much of what goes on remains deliberately hidden from parents and elders. This means that parents think they have more control than they actually have. The irony of this is that because of the sense of biraderi, thinking they have control leads to a sense of real control. The determination to force arranged marriages and to harass those who wish to go their own way, even to the point of murder, shows how deep the control is. The young people resent it, but have to submit to it. This is the deepest of hypocrisies.

The second telling phrase is 'the family should come first'. This is what is ultimately driven into the consciousness of the young. The community looks after its own. Kinship is central. The community both looks after and controls itself. The problem with this, of course, is that it can easily lead to nepotism, to the manipulation of welfare and to dishonest financial arrangements. British society is accused of being immoral, but in terms of 'British' standards nothing could be less moral than the manipulating of a public system of rectitude into personal favours and support. By the standards of kinship, inherited from a different society, many practices that may seem immoral can be justified. The strength of cultural feeling is such that these young people hear the arguments for the support of 'family' and witness them being enacted. They cannot, however, be unaware of the different assumptions made by the society of which they are part. They witness the conflict of two different social and cultural systems.

These young people therefore face all the tensions of hypocrisy and different standards, to a degree which is marked and intense. The question remains as the extent to which they confront this, and the extent to which they can articulate it. That they are able to reveal what actually takes place suggests that they are beginning to adapt to a different way of thinking. They wish to retain Islam, but as written in the Quran, not as a cultural interpretation. One can speculate that the next generation will be culturally distinct and yet completely English.

Bibliography

Aakhus, M. and Katz, J.E. (2002), *Perpetual Contact, Mobile Communication; Private Talk*, Public Performance. Cambridge, Cambridge University Press.

Adams, E. (1988), *Asian Survivors of Domestic Violence*. Norwich, School of Social Work at the University of East Anglia.

Ahmad, W.I.U. (1996), 'The trouble with culture', in *Researching Cultural Differences in Health*, (eds.) D. Kellcher and S. Hillier, pp. 190-219. London, Routledge.

Alibhai-Brown, Y. (1994), 'Sex, veils and stereotypes'. *The Independent*, 22nd December, p. 17.

Allen, S. (1971), *New Minorities Old Conflicts: Asian and West Indian migrants in Britain*, Random House, New York.

Amin, A. (2002), 'Ethnicity and the Multicultural City: Living with Diversity'. Draft Report for the ESRC Cities Programme and the Department of Transport, Local Government and the Regions (DTLR) January.

Annual Local Area Labour Force Survey (2002), London, Office for National Statistics.

Ansari, H. (2004), *"The Infidel Within": Muslims in Britain since 1800*. London, Hurst.

Anwar, M. (1973), 'Pakistani Participation in the 1972 Rochdale By-Election', *New Community*, Vol.2 p. 4.

Anwar, M. (1974), 'Pakistani Participation in the 1973 Local Elections', *New Community*, Vol.3 pp. 1-2.

Anwar, M. (1975), 'Asian Participation in the 1974 Autumn Election', *New Community*, Vol.4 p. 3.

Anwar, M. (1979), *The Myth of Return*, Heinemann, London.

Anwar, M. (1982), *Young Muslims in a Multicultural Society: their needs and policy implications*, The Islamia Foundation, Leicester.

Anwar, M. (1984), *Social and Cultural Perspectives on Muslims in Western Europe*, CSIC, Birmingham.

Anwar, M. (1991a), 'Ethnic Minorities Representation: Voting and Electoral Politics in Britain, and the Role of Leaders', in Werbner, P. and Anwar, M. (eds.), *Black and Ethnic Leaderships*, Routledge, London.

Anwar, M. (1991b), *Race Relations Policies in Britain: Agenda for the 1990s*, Centre for Research in Ethnic Relations, Coventry.

Anwar, M. (1993), *Muslims in Britain: the 1991 Census and Other Statistical Sources*, Birmingham, Centre for the Study of Christian and Muslim Relations, Paper 9.

Anwar, M. (1995), 'New Commonwealth Migration to the UK', in Cohen, R. (ed.), *Cambridge Survey of World Migration*, Cambridge University Press, Cambridge.

Anwar, M. (1996), *British Pakistani: Demographic, Social and Economic Position*, University of Warwick, Centre for Research in Ethnic Relations, Warwick.

Anwar, M. (1998), *Between Cultures, Continuity and Change in the lives of Young Asians*, Routledge, London.

Archer, L. (2003), 'Resisting and surviving: Asian girls and education'. *British Journal of Sociology of Education*, Vol.24 No.5 November, pp. 661-664.

Ashraf, S.A. (1986), 'Foreword' to Halstead, J. M. (1986) *The Case for Muslim Voluntary-Aided Schools: Some Philosophical Reflections*, The Islamic Agency, Cambridge.

Aspinall, P.J. (2003), 'Who is Asian? A category that remains contested in population and health research'. *Journal of Public Health Medicine*, Vol.25 No.2 June, pp. 91-97.

Aurora, G.S. (1967), *The New Frontiersmen: A Sociological Study of Indian Immigrants in the United Kingdom*, Popular Parakashan, Bombay.

Ballard, R. (ed.) (1994), *Desh Pardesh: The South Asian Presence in Britain*, Hurst, London.

Banks, M. (1996), *Ethnicity: Anthropological Constructions*. London, Routledge.

Basit, T. (1997), *Eastern Values; Western Milieu Identities and Aspirations of Adolescent British Muslim Girls*, Ashgate Publishing, Aldershot.

Basit, T. (1997), 'I Want More Freedom, but Not Too Much: British Muslim Girls and the Dynamism of Family Values' (1), *Gender and Education*, Vol.9 No.4, pp. 425-438.

Baumann, G. (1996), *Contesting culture: Discourses of identity in multi-ethnic London*. Cambridge, Cambridge University Press.

Bhat, A. and Ohri, S. (1988), *Britain's Black Population: A New Perspective*. (2nd edition), Gower, Aldershot.

Bhatti, G. (1999), *Asian children at home and at school - an ethnographic study*, Routledge, London.

Bjorgo, T. (2005), Conflict processes between youth groups in a Norwegian City: polarization and revenge. *European Journal of Crime*, Criminal Law and Criminal Justice, Vol.13 No.1 pp. 44-74.

Blair, M. (1994), 'Black Teachers, black students and education markets', *Cambridge Journal of Education*, Vol.24 No2 pp. 277-291.

Bradford Commission (1996), *The Bradford Commission Report*, The Stationery Office, London.

Bradley, S. and Taylor, J. (2001), 'Ethnicity, educational attainment and the transition from school', Department of Economics, Lancaster University, Lancaster.

Bradley, S. and Taylor, J. (2002), 'The effect of the quasi-market on the efficiency-equity trade –off in the secondary school sector', *Bulletin of Economic Research*, 54(3).

Braham, P. et al (ed.) (1992), *Racism, Anti-racism- Inequalities, opportunities and Policies*, Newbury Park California, Sage in association with the Open University, London.

British Muslims' Monthly Survey (1993a), 'Statistics-Muslim Population of Britain: A Short Report', 1(10), pp. 4-5.

Britton, L., Chatrik, B., Coles, G., Hylton, C. and Mumtaz, S. (2002), *Missing ConneXions: The career dynamics and welfare needs of black and minority ethnic young people at the margins*. Joseph Rowntree Foundation.

Brown, C. (1984), 'Black and White in Britain' *The Third PSI Survey*, Policy Studies Institute, London.

Browning, C. (2001), *Ordinary Men*. London, Penguin.

Burnley Task Force (2001), 11th December.

Cabinet Papers (1950), 'Coloured People from British Colonial Territories', (50) 113, Public Records Office.

Cantle, T. (2001), *Community Cohesion: A Report of the Independent Review Team*. Home Office, London.

Carroll, B. and Hollinshead, G. (1993), 'Ethnicity and Conflict in Physical Education', *British Educational Research Journal*, Vol.19 No.1 pp. 59-76.

Chahal, K. (2004), *Experiencing ethnicity: discrimination and service provision*. Joseph Rowntree Foundation.

Condor, S., Gibson, S. and Abell, J. (2005), 'Nations and Regions: Constitutional Change and Identity'. *The Institute of Governance*, University of Edinburgh.

Cosgrave, P. (1990), *The Lives of Enoch Powell*, Pan, London.

Cullingford, C. and Din, I. (2006), *Ethnicity and Englishness: Personal Identities in a Minority Community*. Cambridge Scholars Press, Newcastle.

Dahya, B. (1972-3), 'Pakistanis in England', *New Community*, No.2 pp. 25-33.

Dahya, B. (1974), 'The Nature of Pakistani Ethnicity in Industrial Cities in Britain', in A. Cohen (ed.), *Urban Ethnicity*. Tavistock, London.

Dahya, Z. (1965), 'Pakistani Wives in Britain', *Race*, Vol.VI, No.3 January pp. 311-21.

Davis, S. and Cooke (2002), *Why do Black women organize? A comparative analysis of Black women's voluntary sector organizations in Britain and their relationship to the State*. The Policy Press/Joseph Rowntree Foundation.

Deakin, N. (ed.) (1965), *Colour and the British Electorate*, Pall Mall Press, London.

Deakin, N. (1970), *Colour, Citizenship and the British Society*, Panther, London.

Deaux, K., Reid, A., Mizrahi, K. and Ethier, K.A. (1995) Parameters of social identity. *Journal of Personality and Social Psychology*, Vol.68 No.2 pp. 280-291.

Denham, L. (2001), *Building Cohesive Communities: A Report of the Ministerial Group on Public Order and the Community Cohesion*, Home Office, London.

Desai, R. (1963), *Indian Immigrants in Britain*, Oxford University Press, London.

Din, I. (2001), 'The New British: Generational Change in the Mirpuri Community', PhD unpublished, University of Huddersfield.

Din, I. and Cullingford, C. (2004), 'Boyzone and Bhangra: The place of popular and minority cultures', *Race, Ethnicity and Education*, September, Vol.7 No.3 pp. 307-320.

Din, I. and Cullingford, C. (2005), 'Pakistani Gangs in Schools'. *Race Equality Teaching*, Vol.24 No.1 Autumn pp. 16-19.

Dion, K.K. and Dion, K.L. (2004) 'Gender, immigrant generation and ethno-cultural identity'. *Sex Roles*, Vol.50 Nos.5-6 March, pp. 347-355.

Doi, A.R.I. (1989), *Women in Shari'ah- Islamic Law*, Ta-Ha Publishers, London.

Donald, J. and Rattansi, A. (ed.) (1992), *'Race', Culture and Difference*, Sage Publications, London.

Dooley, P. (1991), 'Muslim Private Schools', in G. Walford (ed.), *Private Schooling: tradition, change and diversity*. Paul Chapman, London.

Dorsett, R. (1998), *Ethnic Minorities in the Inner City*. Bristol, Rowntree.

Dwyer, C. (1999), 'Veiled Meanings: young British Muslim Women and the negotiation of differences'. *Gender, Place and Culture*, Vol.6 No.1 pp. 5-26.

Elahi, K. (1967), 'Some Aspects of Social Adaptation of Pakistani Immigrants in Glasgow', M.A. Thesis, Edinburgh University, Edinburgh.

Emerson, E., Azmi, S., Hatton, C., Parrott, R. and Wolstenholme, J. (1997), 'Is there an increased prevalence of severe learning disabilities among British Asians?' *Ethnicity and Health* Vol.2 No.4 pp. 317-321.

Emerson, E. and Robertson, J. (2002), 'Future demand for services with learning disabilities from South Asian and Black Communities in Birmingham'. *Institute for Health Research*, Lancaster University.

Engels, F. (1952), *The Conditions of the Working Class in England in 1844*, George Allen and Unwin, London.

Fryer, P. (1984), *Staying Power: The History of Black people in Britain*, Pluto Press, London.

Furlong, A. and Cartmel, F. (1997), *Sociology and Social Change Young People and Social Change*, Open University Press, Buckingham.

Furlong, A. and Cartmel, F. (2004), *Vulnerable young men in fragile labour markets: Employment, unemployment and the search for long term security*. Joseph Rowntree Foundation.

Gaine, C. (1995), *Still No Problem Here*, Stoke-on-Trent, Trentham Books, Staffordshire.

Ghuman, P.A.S. (1994), 'Coping with two cultures British Asian and Indo Canadian adolescents', *Multilingual Matters*, Clevedon.

Ghuman, P.A.S. (1999), *Asian Adolescents in the West*, The British Psychological Society, Leicester.

Giampapa, F. (2001), 'Hyphenated identities: Italian-Canadian youth and the negotiation of ethnic identities in Toronto'. *International Journal of Bilingualism*, Vol.5 No.3 September, pp. 279-315.

Gifford, Z. (1990), *The Golden Threat*, Grafton, London.

Gill, D., Mayor, B. and Blair, M. (1992), *Racism and Education Structures and Strategies*, Sage Publications, London.

Gilroy, P. (1987), *There Ain't No Black in the Union Jack: The cultural politics of race and nation*. London, Routledge.

Glatter, R., Woods, P.A. and Bagley, C. (1997), (eds.), *Choice and Diversity in Schooling: Perspectives and Prospects*. Routledge, London.

Glavanis, P.M. (1998), 'Political Islam within Europe: A contribution to an Analytical Framework, "Special Issue on Muslims"'. *Innovation: European Journal of Social Science*, Vol.10 No.4.

Goodall, J. in *New Backgrounds* edited by R. Oakley (1968), Institute of Race Relations, Oxford University Press, Oxford.

Hall, S. (1992), 'New Ethnicities', in J. Donald and A. Rattansi (eds.), *Race, Culture and Difference*, Routledge, London.

Hall, S. (1992a), 'The question of cultural identity' in Stuart Hall, David Held and Ali McGrew (eds.) *Modernity and its Futures*. Cambridge, Polity Press.

Hartley-Brewer, M. (1965), 'Smethwick' in Deakin, N. (ed.), *Colour and the British Electorate 1964*, London, Pall Mall Press.

Hendry, L.B., Shucksmith, J., Love, J.G. and Glendenning, A. (1993), *Young People's Leisure and Lifestyles*, Routledge, London.

Hiro, D. (1991), *Black British, White British: a history or race relations in Britain*, Grafton, London.

Holmes, C. (1991), *A Tolerant Country? Immigrants, Refugees and Minorities in Britain*, Faber, London.

Home Office (2002a), *Secure Borders, Safe Haven: Integration with diversity in modern Britain*, CM5387. The Stationery Office, London.

Hylton, C. (1997), 'Family Survival Strategies' in Moyende S. *Black Families Talking London*, Exploring Parenthood.

Inglehart, R. (1990), Culture Shift in Advanced Industrial Society. New Jersey Princeton University Press.

Islamia: National Muslim Education Newsletter (1994), 'A Muslim Boys Secondary School', No.23, March pp. 6-7.

Iqbal, M. (1975), *Islamic Education and Single Sex Schools*, Union of Muslim Organisations of UK and Eire, London.

Jackson, J.A. (1963), *The Irish in Britain*, Routledge and Kegan Paul, London.

Jacobson, J. (1997), 'Religion and ethnicity: dual and alternative sources of identity among young British Pakistanis'. *Ethnic and Racial Studies*, Vol.20 No.2 pp. 238-56.

Jenkins, R. (1996), "Us" and "Them": Ethnicity, racism and ideology', in R. Barot (ed.), *The Racism Problematic: contemporary Sociological Debates on Race and Ethnicity*. Lewiston, The Edwin Mellen Press.

Jenkins, R. (1997), *Rethinking Ethnicity: Arguments and Exploration*. London, Sage.

Johnson, S. and Burden, T. (2003), *Young people, employability and the induction process*. Joseph Rowntree Foundation.

Kalra, V.S. (2002), 'Extended View: Riots, Race and Reports: Denham, Cantle, Oldham and Burnley Inquiries', Vol.27 No.4 pp. 20-30, Institute of Race Relations.

Kannon, C.T. (1978), 'Cultural adaptation of Asian immigrants-First and Second Generation', Greenford, The Author, 107 Hill Rise, Middlesex.

Karim, I. (1976), *Muslim Children in British Schools: Their Rights and Duties*, The Straight Path, Birmingham.

Khan, V.S. (1974), 'Pakistani Villagers in a British City: the world of the Mirpuri villager in Bradford and his village of origin', unpublished Ph.D. Thesis, University of Bradford.

Khan, V.S. (ed.) (1979), 'Migration and Social Stress: Mirpuris in Bradford', in *Minority Families in Britain, Support and Stress*, MacMillan, London.

Khanum, S. (1992), 'Education and the Muslim girl', in G. Sahgal and N. Yuval-Davis (eds.), *Refusing Holy Orders*. Virago, London.

King, D. (2005), *The Liberty of Strangers: Making the American Nation*. Oxford University Press.

Kondapi, C. (1951), *Indians Overseas 1938-49*. Oxford University Press for Indian Council of World Affairs, New Delhi.

Kroger, J. (1989), *Identity in Adolescence; the balance between self and other*. London, Routledge.

Kundnani, A. (2001), 'From Oldham to Bradford: The Violence of the Violated', *Race and Class* Vol.43 No.2 pp. 105-31.

Layton-Henry, Z. (1992), *The Politics of Immigration*. Blackwell, Oxford.

Lewis, P. (1994), *Islamic Britain*, London, I.B Tauris and Co.

Lucey, H. and Reay, D. (1998), 'Excitement and Anxiety in the Move to Secondary School' (working paper), King's College, London.

Mabud, S.A. (1992), 'A Muslim Response to the Education Reform Act of 1988', *British Journal of Religious Education* (14), pp. 88-98.

Macdonald, J. and Macdonald, L.D. (1962), 'Chain Migration, Ethnic Neighbourhood Formation and Social Network', *Social Research*, 29(4).

MacPherson, W. (1999), 'The Stephen Lawrence Inquiry (The Lawrence Report)', Cm 4262-L. HMSO, London.

Mason, D. (1995), *Race and Ethnicity in Modern Britain*, Oxford University Press, Oxford.

Mason, D. (2000), *Race and Ethnicity in Modern Britain*, (2nd edition), Oxford University Press, Oxford.

McDermot, M.Y. and Ashan, M.M. (1980), *The Muslim Guide*, The Islamic Foundation, London.

Mir, G., Nocon, A., Ahmad, W. And Jones, L. (2001), *Learning Difficulties and Ethnicity*. London, Department of Health.

Modood, T., Berthoud, R., Lakey, J., Nazroo, J., Smith, P., Virdee, S. and Beishon, S. (1997), *Ethnic Minorities in Britain: Diversity and Disadvantage The Fourth National Survey of Ethnic Minorities*, Policy Studies Institute, London.

Mohammad, R. (1999), 'Marginalization, Islamism and the Production of the "Other's" "Other"'. *Gender, Place and Culture*, Vol.6 No.3 pp. 221-240.

Moyenda, S. (1997), *Black Families Talking*. London, Exploring Parenthood.

Nazroo, J.Y. and Karlsen, S. (2003), 'Patterns of identity among ethnic minority: Diversity and commonality'. *Ethnic and Racial Studies*, Vol.26 No.5 September, pp. 902-930.

O'Neill, D. and Cullingford, C (2005), 'Cultural Shock or Cultural Acquisition? The Experiences of Overseas Students' in Cullingford C and Gunn, S *Globalisation and Culture Shock*. Aldershot, Ashgate pp. 107-123.

Oldham Independent Review (2001), 11th December.

Ouseley Report (2001), 'Community Pride Not Prejudice'. Bradford City Council.

Pardesh, D. and Shaw A. (1994), *The South Asian Presence in Britain*, London, Hurst and Co.

Parekh, B. (2000b), 'Defining British National Identity'. *Political Quarterly*, Vol.71 pp. 4-14.

Parker-Jenkins, M. (1991), 'Muslim Matters: An Exploration of the Needs of Muslim Children', *New Community*, Vol.17 No.4, pp. 569-582.

Parker-Jenkins, M. (1995), *Children of Islam: A Teacher's guide to meeting the needs of Muslim pupils*, Trentham Books Ltd, Stoke-on-Trent.

PEP (Political and Economic Planning) (1948), *Population Policy in Great Britain*, PEP, London.

Peterson, W. (1958) 'A General Typology of Migration', *American Sociological Review*, 23.

Price, C. (1969), 'The Study of Assimilation', in J.A. Jackson (ed.), *Migration*, Sociological Studies No.2, Chicago University Press, Chicago.

Ramdin, R. (1999), *Re imaging Britain: five hundred years of Black and Asian History*, Pluto, London.

Ranger, T., Samad, Y. and Stuart, O. (1996), *Culture, Identity and Politics - ethnic minorities in Britain*, Avebury, Aldershot.

Rapoport, R. and Fogarty, M. (ed.) (1982), *Families in Britain*, Routledge and Kegan Paul, London.

Rattansi, A. (2000), 'On being and not being Brown/Black-British: Racism, class, sexuality and ethnicity in post-imperial Britain'. *Interventions: international Journal of Postcolonial Studies*, Vol.2 No.1 March, pp. 118-134.

Raza, M.S. (1991), *Islam in Britain, Past, Present and Future*, Volcano, Leicester.

Raza, M.S. (1993), *Islam in Britain, Past, Present and Future*, (2nd edition), Volcano, Leicester.

Reay, D. (1998), 'Engendering and social reproduction: mothers in the educational marketplace', *British Journal of Sociology of Education*, Vol.19 No.2, pp. 195-209.

Reyes, A. (2005), 'Appropriation of African American slang by Asian American youth'. *Journal of Sociolinguistics*, Vol.9 No.4 November, pp. 509-532.

Rich, P.B. (1994), *Prospero's Return*, Atlansib Publications, London.

Ringmer, E. (1998), 'Nationalism: the Idiocy of Intimacy'. *British Journal of Sociology* Vol. 49 No. 4 pp. 534-549.

Robinson, F. (1993), *Separatism among Indian Muslims the politics of the United Provinces Muslims 1860-1923*, Delhi, Oxford University Press, London.

Rose, E.J.B. with Deakin, N., Abrams, M., Jackson, V., Peston, M., Vanags, A.H., Cohen, B., Gaitskell, J., and Ward, P. (1969), *Colour and Citizenship*, Oxford University Press for Institute of Race Relations, London.

Royal Commission on Population (1949), 'Report of the Royal Commission on Population', Cmmd 7695, HMSO, London.

Salih, R. (2004), 'The backward and the New: National, trans-national and post-national Islam in Europe'. *Journal of Ethnic and Migration Studies*, Vol.30 No.5 pp. 995-1011.

Samad, Y. (2004), 'Muslim Youth in Britain: Ethnic to Religious Identity'. Paper presented at the International Conference: Muslim Youth in Europe, Typologies of religious belonging and socio-cultural dynamics, Edoardo Agnelli Centre for Comparative Religious Studies. Turin, 11th June 2004.

Sarwar, M. (1980), *Islam, Beliefs and Teachings*. London, The Muslim Educational Trust.

Sarwar, M. (1983), *Muslims and Education in the UK*, Muslim Educational Trust, 130 Stroud Green Road, London, N4 3AZ, London.

Sarwar, M. (1994), *British Muslims and Schools*, Muslim Educational Trust 130 Stroud Green Road, London, N4 3AZ, London.

Scantlebury, E. (1995), 'Muslims in Manchester: the depiction of a religious community'. *New Community*, Vol.18 pp. 425-435.

Shaw, A. (1988), *A Pakistani Community in Britain*, Blackwell, Oxford.

Shaw, A. (1994), 'The Pakistani Community in Oxford', in R. Ballard (ed.), *Desh Pardesh: The South Asian Presence in Britain*. Hurst, London.

Skellington, R., Paulette, M. and Paul, G. (1996), *Race*, (2nd edition), Sage Publications, London.

Skjonsberg, E. (1982), *A Special Caste? Tamil women of Sri Lanka*, (2nd edition), Zed, London.

Smaje, C. (1996), 'The ethnic patterning of health: new directions for theory and research'. *Sociology of Health and Illness*, Vol.18 No.2 pp. 139-171.

Smith, G. (1990), 'The Next Ten Years', *Muslim Educational Quarterly*, Vol.1 No.5, pp. 26-27.

Social Exclusion Unit (July 1999), *Bridging the Gap: New Opportunities for 16-18 year olds not in Education, Employment or Training*, HMSO, London.

Social Trends 30 (2000), HMSO, London.

Solomos, J. (1998), 'Beyond racism and multi-culturalism'. *Patterns of Prejudice*, Vol.32 No.4 pp. 45-62.

Stopes-Roe, M. E. and Cochrane, R. (1990), 'Citizens of this country - the Asian-British', *Multilingual Matters*, Clevedon.

Swann, M. (1985), *Education for All: A Summary of the Swann Report on the Education of Ethnic Minority Children*, NFER-Nelson, Windsor.

Taylor, J. (1976), *The half way generation, a study of Asian youths in Newcastle-Upon-Tyne*, NFER, Windsor.

Taylor, M. and Hegarty, S. (1985), *The Best of Both Worlds...? A Review of Research into the Education of Pupils of South Asian Origin*, NFER-Nelson, Windsor.

Thornton, S. (1995), *Club Cultures- Music, Media and Sub cultural Capital*, Polity Press, Cambridge.

Tomlinson, S. (1984), *Home and School in Multicultural Britain*. Batsford, London.

Tomlinson, S. (1997), 'Diversity, Choice and ethnicity: the effects of educational markets on ethnic minorities', *Oxford Review of Education*, Vol.23 No.1, pp. 63-76.

Varshney, A. (2002), *Ethnic Conflict and Civic Life: Hindus and Muslims in India*. Hew Haven, Yale University Press.

Vernon, A. (2002), *User-defined outcomes of community care for Asian disabled people*. The Policy Press/Joseph Rowntree Foundation.

Visram, R.C. (1986), *Ayahs, Lascars and Princes*, Pluto Press, London.

Walseth, K. (2006), 'Young Muslim women and sport: the impact of identity'. *Leisure Studies*, Vol.25 No.1 January, pp. 75-94.

Warikoo, N. (2005), 'Gender and ethnic identity among second-generation Caribbeans'. *Ethnic and Racial Studies*, Vol.28 No.5 September, pp. 803-831.

Watson, J. (1977), *Between Two Cultures: migrants and minorities in Britain*. Oxford, Basil Blackwell.

Watson, S. (1997), 'Single-sex education for girls: heterosexuality, gendered subjectivity and school choice', *British Journal of Education*, Vol.18 No.3, pp. 371-383.

Werbner, P. (1990), *The Migration Process: Capital, Gifts and Offerings among British Pakistanis*, Berg, Oxford.

Werbner, P. (2002), *Imagined Diasporas among Manchester Muslims: The Public Performance of Pakistani Transnational Identity Politics*, School of American Research Press, Oxford.

Werbner, P. and Anwar, M. (1991), (eds.), *Black and Ethnic Leaderships*, Routledge, London.

Wrench, J. and Solomos, J. (ed.) (1993), *Racism and Migration in Western Europe*, Berg, Oxford.

Wright, R. (2002), *Patriots: National Identity in Britain 1940-2000*. Macmillan, London.

Author Index

Subject Index